WHAT EVERY ENGINEER SHOULD KNOW ABOUT MICROCOMPUTER SYSTEMS DESIGN AND DEBUGGING

WHAT EVERY ENGINEER SHOULD KNOW
A Series

Editor

William H. Middendorf

Department of Electrical and Computer Engineering
University of Cincinnati
Cincinnati, Ohio

Other volumes in preparation

WHAT EVERY ENGINEER SHOULD KNOW ABOUT MICROCOMPUTER SYSTEMS DESIGN AND DEBUGGING

Bill Wray and Bill Crawford

Motorola Microsystems
Tempe, Arizona

MARCEL DEKKER, INC.   New York and Basel

Wray, William C.
What every engineer should know about microcomputer
systems design and debugging.

(What every engineer should know ; v. 12)
Includes index.
1. Debugging in computer science. 2. Microcomputers
—Design and construction. 3. Microcomputers—
Programming. I. Crawford, Bill, [date]. II. Title.
III. Title: Microcomputer system design and debugging.
IV. Series.
QA76.6.W73   1984   001.64   83-25204
ISBN 0-8247-7160-5

Marcel Dekker, Inc.
270 Madison Avenue, New York, New York 10016

Current printing (last digit):
10 9 8 7 6 5 4 3 2 1

Printed in the United States of America

PREFACE

By now most engineers have heard of the significant advances being made in semiconductor electronics. Many articles have been written describing the microcomputer revolution now taking place. The availability of a wide variety of microcomputer components, at attractively low prices, has produced revolutionary changes in all manufacturing and industrial control processes.

Because of the drastic reductions in the cost of this type of programmable logic, many tasks formerly achieved by mechanical, hydraulic, fluidic, or pneumatic means can now be accomplished more effectively and reliably using these electronic devices.

This opens a whole new world of machines and systems that are practical and possible. Application of microcomputers to all aspects of business and industry has resulted in direct competition with nonelectronic devices of all types.

Many nonelectronic engineers are confused by the microprocessor. They often view it as a mysterious device that they will never understand. In reality, many of these engineers have been designing mechanical controllers that are programmable and that use logic concepts, which are basically the same as that provided in a microcomputer system. These include such things as interlocking levers or relays (where one inhibits the other, or where two have to operate together). This logic can be implemented in a microcomputer system with standard software instructions.

Engineers sometimes hesitate to replace present controllers with microcomputers because they think they will have difficulties translating the original design to a microcomputer design. They fear they will have great difficulty not only in knowing which electronic devices to use, but figuring out how to use the software and test or debug the new design. This hesitancy may exist whether the design being replaced is mechanical or electronic (using traditional digital semiconductor devices).

One of our goals in writing this book has been to clarify some of the details of determining whether a microcomputer system is appropriate, and, if so, to help understand the problems of designing and debugging such a system. The details of interconnecting the components of a microcomputer are not covered but rather a modular approach is used which is more easily followed by nonelectronic engineers.

Specifically, Chapter 1 describes the basics of computers with simple descriptions of the parts. Chapter 2 covers the evaluation processes and factors governing the decision to assemble a microcomputer for the job in mind. Chapter 3 describes a simple control system that we have chosen to use as an example. The tools used to help in the design and testing are described in Chapter 4, with the explanation of the role of software, and its debugging included in Chapter 5. The final system test techniques are developed in Chapter 6.

Since the book is devoted primarily to simple explanations of debugging methods, it should help alleviate some of the fears that many nonelectronic engineers may have about this seemingly mysterious process.

The authors have spent many years answering questions from both qualified and novice potential users of microcomputers, so we can provide much useful material. "Computer jargon" has been avoided as much as possible, but where it was unavoidable, the words have been *italicized* when first introduced. These italicized words have been collected in a glossary with explanations for quick reference, in case the meaning has been forgotten.

Since both of the authors are employed at Motorola Microsystems, and are most familiar with Motorola's Micromodules and EXORciser Development Systems, we may therefore frequently refer to them.

We would like to acknowledge that many of the terms used in the text are trademarks of Motorola Inc. These include EXORcisor®, EXbug, MDOS, EXORdisk, and Micromodule.

We hope that our readers will be inspired enough to delve further into the world of microcomputer electronics.

Bill Wray
Bill Crawford

CONTENTS

WHAT EVERY ENGINEER SHOULD KNOW ABOUT MICROCOMPUTER SYSTEMS DESIGN AND DEBUGGING

CHAPTER 1
INTRODUCTION

We will assume that many of our readers are engineers who are looking at the possibilities of using Microcomputers to replace other control techniques in Industrial Controllers. Even if you do not fit that description, and are interested in microcomputer systems design and debugging for other reasons you will undoubtedly find information of interest in the following chapters.

One of the first requirements in converting mechanical controllers to a microcomputer design is to provide the electromechanical interfaces. Once the mechanical action can be controlled by an electrical signal, using solenoids or motors, and the performance can be monitored by electrical sensors, the microcomputer can be used. The functional control sequences previously used in the mechanical design can then be translated to computer instructions.

Before pursuing the conversion to microcomputer control, it is necessary to understand how a microcomputer system functions and how it can control the necessary electro-mechanical interfaces. It will be assumed that the reader has read other books on Micro-computers such as Volume 3 of this series, "What Every Engineer Should Know About Microcomputers". The following, hopefully, will add to that knowledge.

MICROCOMPUTER COMPONENTS

A microcomputer, like any computer, consists of four basic parts:

1. The Central Processing Unit (CPU) — the decision making and control unit, or in the case of the microcomputer, the MicroProcessing Unit (MPU).

2. The Read Only Memory (ROM) — which holds the controlling program. It is manufactured with a fixed set of user-defined instructions and/or data. Alternatively, an Electrically Programmable Read Only Memory (EPROM) can be used, and is sometimes preferred, since it can be erased and reprogrammed.

3. The Random Access Memory (RAM) — used for

temporary storage of data. This is a very confusing name since ROM is also random access memory. However, the RAM contents can be instantly or dynamically changed and therefore is universally known as read/write memory.

4. The Input/Output (I/O) units—which provide the interfacing between the internal microcomputer devices and the external hardware.

These four elements of a computer (see Figure 1.1) can all be implemented in semiconductor devices and several, or all of them, may be included in one *chip*. The various semi-

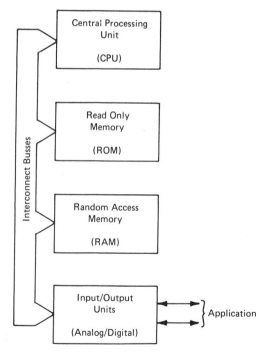

Figure 1.1 Microcomputer Diagram

conductor manufacturers usually provide a set of compatible components which are known as a *family* of chips. The functions provided by different manufacturers are very similar and the families can be intermixed in some cases.

Digital Microcomputers

The type of computer implemented with microcomputer chips is known as a *digital* computer. This refers to the fact that information used by this type of computer is in *binary* or *two-state* form. The input or output signals that are present on the electrical terminals or *pins* of the microcomputer parts are either *full* voltage or *no* voltage. Since most microcomputers are designed to work with a 5 volt power supply, full voltage is 5 volts. Actually, one of the reasons why digital computers are so reliable is that these signal levels do not have to be very accurate. A voltage between 2.0 and 5.25 volts is considered to be in the *HIGH* state and a voltage between 0 and 0.8 volts is *LOW*. A HIGH is also known as a **1** level and a LOW as a **0** level. [These are commonly referred to as *TTL signal* or *logic levels* (see Figure 1.2).]

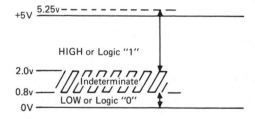

Figure 1.2 Microcomputer Logic Levels

Number Systems

When these HIGH and LOW states are present on the pins of a microcomputer, or other family chip (such as a RAM or ROM), the internal circuitry will treat the information as **1's** or **0's**. These **1's** and **0's** are known as binary digits or *bits*. A typical binary number is 11010011. Just as in decimal numbers the relative position of the digits is important (01 and 10 for example). In decimal we have the *ones, tens,* or *hundreds* columns, while in binary we have the *ones, twos, fours,* etc. For example:

$$10^2 \ 10^1 \ 10^0 \qquad\qquad 2^7 \ 2^6 \ 2^5 \ 2^4 \ 2^3 \ 2^2 \ 2^1 \ 2^0$$
$$1 \ \ 5 \ \ 6 \qquad\qquad\quad 1 \ 0 \ 0 \ 1 \ 1 \ 1 \ 0 \ 0$$

$$
\begin{aligned}
156 = \ & 1 \times 10^2 = 100 \\
+ & 5 \times 10^1 = \ \ 50 \\
+ & 6 \times 10^0 = \underline{\ \ \ \ 6} \\
& \qquad\qquad 156
\end{aligned}
\qquad
\begin{aligned}
10011100 = \ & 1 \times 2^7 = 128 \\
+ & 1 \times 2^4 = \ \ 16 \\
+ & 1 \times 2^3 = \ \ \ \ 8 \\
+ & 1 \times 2^2 = \underline{\ \ \ \ 4} \\
& \qquad\qquad 156
\end{aligned}
$$

The *weight* of each decimal column is related to the powers of ten, while the binary bit positions are related to powers of two. If we look at the two columns of addition, it can be seen that the eight binary digit numbers (10011100) in the example, is equivalent to decimal 156.

Although the computer understands binary numbers without difficulty, it is hard for humans to deal with them. For that reason, other number systems such as *octal* (base 8), or *hexadecimal* (base 16) are frequently used by programmers. Since microcomputers use groups of 8 or 16 binary bits to represent data or addresses, and these easily translate to 2 or 4 hexadecimal (called hex) digits, it is standard practice to use the hexadecimal numbering system in discussing microcomputer information.

9   C

1001   1100

If the previous binary number 10011100 is separated, as shown above, into two four-bit groups (1001 and 1100), it can be seen from Table 1.1, that 1001 = 9 and 1100 = C therefore, 10011100 in binary is equivalent to the hexadecimal number 9C. It should also be noted how easy the translation from binary to hexadecimal becomes, and how hexadecimal numbers are useful to simplify information since one hex digit is equal to two decimal or four binary digits.

A dollar sign (**$**) is used in the rest of this book to indicate hexidecimal numbers (**$E3** for example), and a percent sign (**%**) is used for binary numbers. (**%11100011**). Decimal numbers will not be given a prefix. Note that hex and decimals numbers below 10 (0 to 9) have the same value and therefore do not need a prefix. Also note that 1234 is not the same value as $1234.

Binary Representation

To represent these values electrically, in their binary form, as will be the case in the microcomputer, we could wire up a row

TABLE 1.1

Number Systems Conversion Chart

Decimal	Binary	Hexadecimal
0	0000	0
1	0001	1
2	0010	2
3	0011	3
4	0100	4
5	0101	5
6	0110	6
7	0111	7
8	1000	8
9	1001	9
10	1010	A
11	1011	B
12	1100	C
13	1101	D
14	1110	E
15	1111	F

of switches and turn ON those that represent **1's** and turn OFF those that represent **0's**, as shown in Figure 1.3. This is essentially what is done in semiconductor memories, except that a *logic element* is turned ON or OFF. This logic element can take several forms but details of them are not essential to the understanding of this concept.

Each memory location in effect contains eight *logic elements* which are *SET* for a 1 or *RESET* for a **0** to represent the stored value. Groups of eight bits are called *bytes* and can be represented by two hex digits. The RAM (read/write) memory has many of these locations, each with its eight bits, which

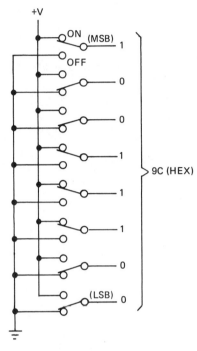

Figure 1.3 Binary Representation

can be changed electrically when *writing* to an addressed location. Reading the value does not change it. A ROM (Read-Only–Memory) has the bits permanently fixed in a programmed pattern when it is manufactured. The EPROM can be programmed electrically (bits SET) but can only be erased or cleared (all RESET) by means of an ultra-violet light. It holds the bit pattern, even with the power removed, for up to ten years. It should be pointed out that the *registers* in a microprocessor function the same as RAM memory locations and they store 8 or 16 bits of data in the same way.

Many of us are familiar with post offices where letters are filed in orderly numbered pigeon-holes. We can use this analogy to describe a block of memory. Let us imagine that the pigeon-holes are numbered hexadecimally. We start with zero (0), and increment from bottom to top and from left to right as shown in Figure 1.4.

Also imagine that the block of memory is three-dimensional. That is, each box or location has an address and room inside for eight bits of information or data. The bits are binary bits and are either a **1** or a **0**. Thus each box or location (which has a unique *address*), can store a byte of data. When a byte is placed in one of the locations, for example, it is said to be *loaded* or *stored* into memory. Many Integrated Circuit (IC) memory *chips* are organized in this fashion. They are known as *byte-wide* memories since they hold 8-bits at each memory location. The smallest practical block of RAM of this type in a separate IC is 128 bytes × 8-bits. The largest RAM block available in a single IC is currently about 2048 bytes × 8. These in-

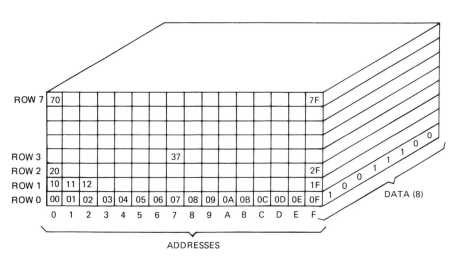

Figure 1.4 128 Byte × 8-Bit Memory Block

dividual ICs contain not only the memory cells, but also the necessary interfacing circuitry. Other sizes of RAM memory blocks are easily built using a group of separate ICs. Instead of byte-wide arrangements, these chips are organized differently. They can be thought of as columns or one bit. Therefore eight are required to make a byte-wide memory. They are currently available in several popular sizes (1-bit × 4096, 1-bit × 16384, or even 1-bit × 65536). Thus an 8-bit × 65536 byte block of memory can be assembled with just 8 of these memory ICs. However, additional chips are needed to input and output the data bits and to decode the addresses (see Figure 1.5). ROMs and EPROMs commonly used are byte-wide and are available in 1024, 2048, 4096, 8192 and 16384 byte blocks (up to 131072 or 128K bits).

MICROCOMPUTER INTERFACES

Microprocessors, and many Input/Output (I/O) devices, also have byte-wide locations to store data. These temporary storage locations are known as registers. For example, when a microprocessor performs a *read* operation, data is brought into an MPU register, and when a *write* occurs, data is sent out of an MPU register to the external bus.

Although external devices which are being controlled frequently use just one signal wire (and ground) for an ON/OFF function, the signals within the microcomputer are usually carried on eight line buses (i.e., information is moved between the microcomputer components as a *parallel* byte). Many reasons exist for this choice and most are beyond the scope of this book but a simple explanation is that 8 parallel lines can move

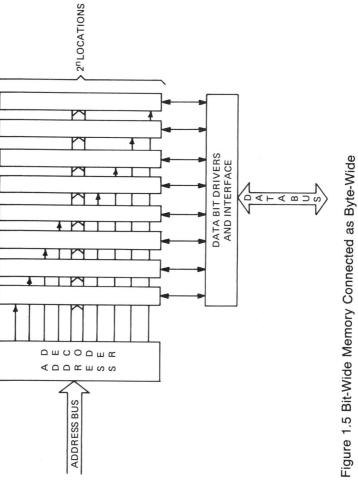

Figure 1.5 Bit-Wide Memory Connected as Byte-Wide

information faster. Several peripheral interface devices are available to transfer the internal 8-bit data to these external control signal lines.

Each microprocessor family includes a number of I/O devices for interfacing to external equipment. For example, the Peripheral Interface Adapter (PIA) is used for *parallel* I/O. The PIA has two byte-wide data registers that can be configured to work either as input or as output registers. The registers in the PIA are similar to memory locations except that each bit of the data register has an IC pin associated with it. When programmed as an output, bytes written to the register will cause the pins on the IC to be raised to the HIGH level (2.0 to 5.25 volts) or taken LOW (0 to 0.8 volts), depending on whether the bits are **1**'s or **0**'s. Thus, when a byte is written to the PIA data register, the voltages on the IC pins change to values which correspond to the state of the bits. See Figure 1.6.

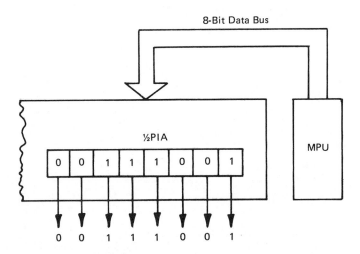

Figure 1.6 PIA Register

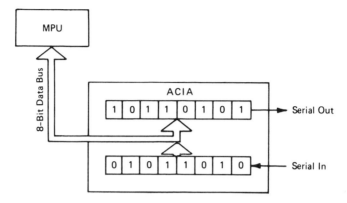

Figure 1.7 ACIA Registers

The Asynchronous Communications Interface Adapter (ACIA), is used for *serial* I/O. The ACIA inputs data serially from a single line into one register where it is available as a parallel byte to the microcomputer's internal bus. Another data register in the ACIA accepts parallel data bytes from the microcomputer and outputs them as serial bits over one wire to an external device. See Figure 1.7.

SYSTEM CONCEPTS

The classic approach when designing a microcomputer controller is to provide only the simplest interface such that when the signal is ON (or + 5 V), the motor runs, the valve is opened, or the light is lit, and when it is zero volts they are OFF. All interlocking, limiting, or latching functions are delegated to the microcomputer and its software logic. This technique frequently results in a design with minimum hardware cost. If the microprocessor can handle all tasks in the time allocated this could result in the most cost effective approach. However, it is possible that running the software routines takes too much time (it could take milliseconds which is a very long time for a microcomputer), or that an all electronic system could be construed as not being fail-safe (because, for example, something might not get turned off due to electrical failure). In these events the designer might find that by including some hardware logic in the form of a timer, an overload breaker, or limit switch the processor tasks can be reduced appreciably or the safety is improved. The job then becomes one of analysis of mechanical costs vs. electronic costs with weights being given to safety, and other hardware/software tradeoffs. Remember however, that electronic devices can be more reliable than mechanical ones because they do not wear out.

The final design is arrived at by a careful review of all factors. If the control of the machine being built is done with a microcomputer and its software, instead of by other traditional means, the microcomputer could provide more features, be more flexible, be more reliable and also should cost less. It probably will exhibit some combination of all these benefits.

A traditional control system, designed with electro-mechanical hardware such as switches, relays, timers etc., is normally designed for a specific application. If the application requirements change or a new application is required, the control system hardware must be rewired or rebuilt or both. In a microcomputer based control system major changes in system functions can usually be accomodated in the software, many times with no hardware changes being required.

When a microcomputer system is designed, the software (or programming) costs can become appreciable. These costs are one time costs, however, and can be amortized over the full production life of the product. Also, proper attention to the use of fully capable microcomputer development tools can keep these costs down by reducing the development time.

Many of the pieces of a microcomputer system can be treated as separate sub-systems. A variety of these sub-systems in the form of *modular* building block boards or cards are available from many sources. They can be used to assemble computer controllers or processors, thus eliminating the need for the system designers to be involved in the detailed design of the digital electronic hardware on each Printed Circuit (PC) card. A complete system is sometimes assembled on a single PC card using companion RAM, ROM, or I/O units which form the family of ICs (see Figure 1.8). These cards are referred to as a Single Board Computer (SBC). These are not necessarily simply systems but, in any case, can be expanded in capability by adding other boards with still more memory or I/O chips.

The interconnecting lines between the functional blocks are referred to as the *address bus* (usually 16 wires or lines), the *data bus* (usually 8 lines), and the *control bus* (possibly 9 or so lines). See Figure 1.8. When the system is made up of individual ICs, these interconnecting lines are typically the tracks on a printed circuit board. But, in larger systems, where the functions are placed on separate modular boards, the buses include lines between PC board connectors on a *Motherboard*.

It is not our intention to describe how to design a microcomputer system from scratch, or to deal with interconnecting

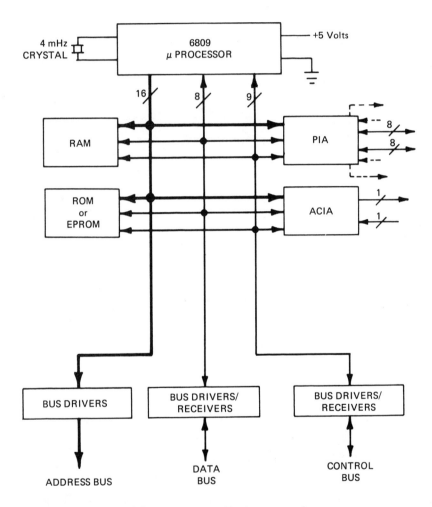

Figure 1.8 Typical Microcomputer System

individual ICs, but instead, to show how to configure a system with modular sub-system assemblies and, more importantly, how to *debug* the system in an orderly, sequential fashion.

There are many similarities between microcomputer families of parts made by various manufacturers. There are also many reasons which may make one family choice desireable. The information given here is applicable in most cases to all systems of this type.

CHAPTER 2
CONSIDERATIONS
FOR SYSTEM
IMPLEMENTATION

There are essentially three major steps or processes that an engineer must go through between the first awareness of the potential application of microprocessors to a given task and the final completion of the microcomputer system. These three steps are:

1. The Evaluative Process

2. The Design Verification Process

3. The Detailed Design Process

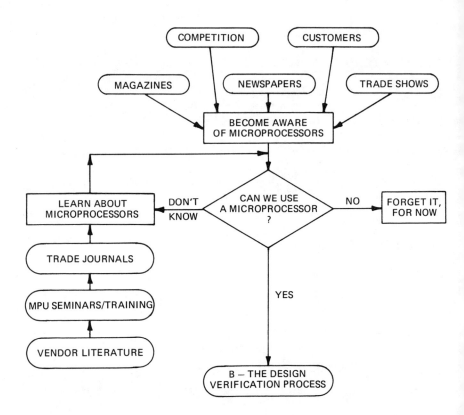

Figure 2.1 The Evaluative Process

THE EVALUATIVE
PROCESS (Figure 2.1)

Once the engineer has become aware of the potential uses of microprocessors, the next step is to determine if a microcomputer system can be used to perform the specific application. This decision requires that the design engineer either be or become familiar with the capabilities of microcomputers. These include monitoring data, doing calculations, making decisions, and outputting control signals. Most process control systems are readily handled by a microcomputer system. Occasionally, however, there may be some system constraint that will preclude the use of a microprocessor such as the need for extremely high-speed, high-precision calculations. In this case the designer may decide that a microcomputer can not handle the job. However, he should note that continuous progress is being made in microcomputer technology and higher performance devices are being announced every day. Also, it is possible that the high speed function can be handled with separate bipolar integrated circuitry and the microcomputer can do all the other functions.

In case the design engineer either doesn't know or is just not sure about the use of a microprocessor for his application, there are a number of ways to learn more about them. Many excellent books have been written on the subject. The trade journals have numerous articles on microprocessors every month and all of the microprocessor venders offer training classes. Application notes and literature describing the products are also readily available. Any design engineer considering the use of microprocessors should avail himself of these resources.

Once the decision has been made that a microcomputer can be used, the next step can be taken.

THE DESIGN VERIFICATION PROCESS (Figure 2.2)

This step requires a higher level of expertise. If the company has the required in-house design talent available to analyze the system design requirements then this is by far the more preferable way to go. These "in-house people" would have more detailed knowledge of, or easier access to, the specifics of the application. If this talent is not available then in-house people must be trained or an outside consultant must be hired to assist in the design. The Design Verification Process results in the selection of a microprocessor *chip set* that can be used to implement a viable hardware/software system design. The system designers must look at:

1. The microprocessor chip family capabilities.

2. The availability of various peripheral support chips (required to interface to the external system).

3. The availability and capability of the development system hardware and software.

4. The possibility of using off-the-shelf hardware to construct the system.

5. System level software requirements, i.e., can or

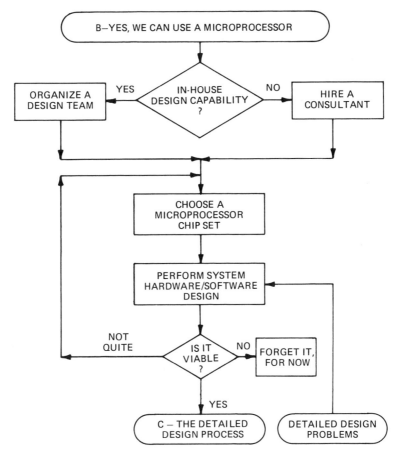

Figure 2.2 The Design Verification Process

should a high level language such as Basic or Fortran be used to implement the software?

Proper considerations of all these elements will determine if a practical design can be implemented. Once that decision has been made the designers can proceed to the next step.

**THE DETAILED
DESIGN PROCESS**
(Figure 2.3)

The Detailed Design Process starts with a make/buy decision. Some of the factors that should be considered are:

1. Does your company have the talent and resources required to design, lay out, and manufacture your own microprocessor system boards? Can better use be made of this talent and these resources?

2. Does the system require a size or shape or combination of elements that are not available in standard off-the-shelf modular products?

3. Can your company afford the additional time required to design, develop and debug the classic "Disaster Sandwich" shown in Figure 2.4? This inevitably results from attempting to use unproven hardware, with a newly built system interface, sandwiched around untested software.

4. Which approach is more cost effective for the number of systems to be produced when you consider all of the various cost elements?

Cost Analysis

The results of the make/buy decision can be illustrated in an unquantified form (see Figure 2.5). The actual numbers that result from such an analysis will vary widely from company

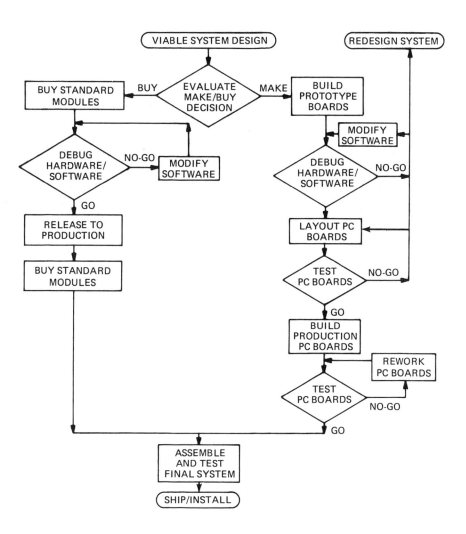

Figure 2.3 The Detailed Design Process

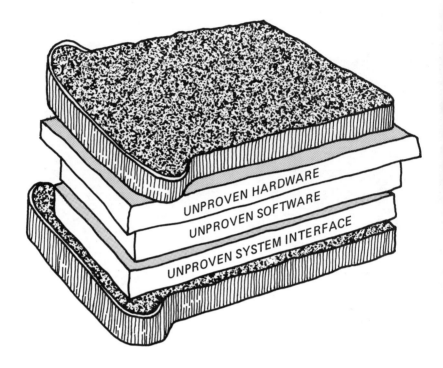

Figure 2.4 Disaster Sandwich

to company. However, history has shown that the crossover point of the make vs buy curves is around 500 or more units. The typical board development costs should be considered as a function of time, including an *opportunity cost* factor that is frequently overlooked. Opportunity costs are those indirect costs associated with the time it takes to complete the design. These costs include:

1. The loss due to the use of personnel and other resources that could be better utilized elsewhere.

2. The losses due to market timing (if this is to be a saleable product).

3. The cost of delays in applying the system if it is for in-house use.

The designer can plot the cost comparison between the *make* or *buy standard hardware* approach. The cost of software has been assumed to be the same in both cases. However, it normally takes longer and is potentially more difficult to develop software for a *non-standard* hardware design. This is the case if the new hardware cannot take full advantage of the Development System capabilities as described in Chapters 4 and 5.

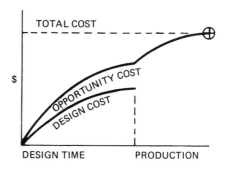

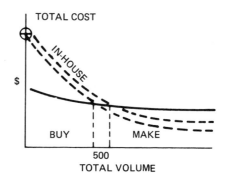

Figure 2.5 Make/Buy Analysis

Even when the make/buy decision favors a make-it-yourself plan, it is a good idea to build the first prototype system with off-the-shelf modules. Working with known hardware will speed and simplify the initial test and debug phase. Once this prototype system is operational, the final decision can be made as to whether the time and costs of translating the design to a more desirable module size or to a lower cost design (in the long run), is worthwhile.

HARDWARE SELECTION

In selecting the hardware that best matches the system requirements, there are two situations that must be considered:

1. A totally new system where both the end application and the microprocessor control system are being designed at the same time.

2. An existing system where manual or semi-automatic control is being replaced by a microprocessor control system.

New System Design

In this case, the system designer has the option of selecting the application hardware, and can choose hardware that is directly interfaceable with the microprocessor. For example, a flow valve that accepts TTL control signals and provides its position information in TTL level digital form can be simply connected.

Existing System Design

If an existing system is to be monitored and controlled then the designer may have to add additional hardware to properly interface that system to the new microprocessor design. For example, if the system requires any AC or high voltage DC control signals, then some type of level translating and possibly isolation circuitry will be required. Any *analog* signal requirements will require the use of Analog-to-Digital (A/D), or Digital-to-Analog (D/A) converter modules. These additional modules are all available for microcomputer uses but obviously, will add hardware costs and may complicate some of the system software thus also increasing its cost.

Analyzing Design Requirements

The step-by-step procedures for analyzing the design requirements of this system are:

1. Looking at the system's overall requirements to determine if a microprocessor based system can be used and if so what the system interfaces will be. In the example system to be used in this book (See Figure 2.6), the system requirements are:

   A. Monitor and control the performance of a heater system based on parameters established and communicated to the control system by the main plant computer system.

   B. In order to minimize the plant wiring, the control system should be physically located near the heater.

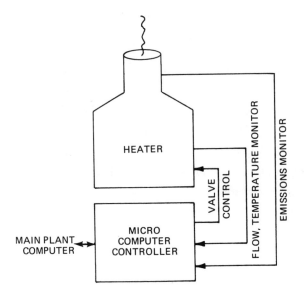

Figure 2.6 Application Example

C. For purposes of illustration, this is considered to be a new system and therefore the heater hardware can be selected to provide a simplified, direct interface between the heater and the control system.

D. The system software algorithms will:

a. Control the fuel/oxygen flow rates to adjust the temperature to the *setpoint* value received over the communications link from the main plant computer.

b. Monitor the combustion emissions.

c. Balance the fuel/oxygen ratio to keep the exhaust emissions at an acceptable level.

In other words, this system and its software program must be capable of maintaining the required temperature while maximizing system efficiency and minimizing the exhaust emissions. Clearly this application requires a computer function that can be met by a microcomputer system.

2. The system interfaces must be defined so that the proper microcomputer hardware can be selected. In this example (see Table 2.1) these interfaces are between the microcomputer subsystem being designed, and:

A. The main plant computer — To be provided by a serial communications interface.

B. The fuel and oxygen valves — For control and monitoring. Valves can be selected that can be

TABLE 2.1

Example System Interfaces

Function	Signal
Plant Computer	Serial data
Valve Control	TTL Level
Flow Monitor	TTL Level
Temperature	Thermocouple
Emissions	TTL Parallel
Control Panel	Serial Data

controlled by TTL level signals eliminating the need for any level translating hardware (if this proves to be most cost effective).

C. **Fuel and oxygen flow meters** — Meters can be selected that output a series of TTL level pulses that indicate the rate of flow of the fuel and the oxygen.

D. **A temperature measuring thermocouple** — *Thermocouples* exhibit three difficulties that must be overcome. First, when the thermocouple leads are connected to the copper leads in the system a second thermocouple effect is generated that must be compensated for. Second, the thermocouple output is a low-level analog signal, (in the millivolt range), and must therefore be amplified prior to conversion to digital representation. Finally, a thermocouple generates a non-linear output as a function of temperature and therefore must be linearized. These problems can be solved two different ways. A thermocouple preamplifier which includes *cold-junction* compensation for the undesired thermocouple effect can be used, with the linearization being done in software. This approach adds both hardware costs and software complexity. The other solution would be to use an analog-to-digital converter that provides both cold-junction compensation and low-level signal capability as well as linearization for the required type of the thermocouple.

E. An emission analyzer — one can be selected that outputs its data in a digital, TTL level, parallel word format.

F. Local front-panel — provides displays and manual controls for use by the plant operating engineer in emergencies.

3. The economic trade-offs of selecting the *best-cost* combinations of system hardware and microcomputer hardware along with the make/buy decision must be analyzed. Since the primary purpose of this book involves system debugging techniques and not detailed system design techniques, we have chosen to implement our design with standard, off-the-shelf microcomputer modules. An 8-bit family of board level products has been selected which includes all of the elements required to implement this design. Such products are available from a number of vendors.

CHAPTER 3
A TYPICAL
MICROCOMPUTER
INDUSTRIAL
CONTROL SYSTEM

The chemical plant heater control system referenced in Chapter 2 is an example of system design and will be used to demonstrate debugging techniques.

Microprocessor control is used to obtain the best possible fuel efficiency and at the same time to keep the combustion emissions at the lowest level. In this system, the fuel/oxy-

35

gen mixture is regulated by electrically controlled valves, and the exhaust emissions are determined by a gas analyzer. The temperature of the heater is monitored and maintained by this control sub-system to the value specified by the main plant computer. This microcomputer design is known as a *closed loop* control system since it is self-regulating. See Figure 3.1.

In order to implement the electronic microcomputer control provided by this subsystem, it is necessary to gather information about how the heater is performing and to change the fuel and oxygen flow, if necessary, to maintain proper operation. Typically, electro-mechanical valves will be used to control the fuel and oxygen flow. Thermocouples and other electrical sensors will be used for gathering performance information.

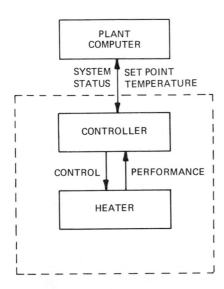

Figure 3.1 Heater Control System

As mentioned previously, it is not our intention to go into the detailed design of the microcomputer circuitry and associated Integrated Circuits (ICs) required for this job, but to use a building block approach using modular system components. There are many modules available from a number of vendors that could provide the functions required. Since we needed to be specific for this example, we have selected Motorola's Micromodule family because they include the system functions we need.

System Requirements

The heater control system to be described will require a software program which scans the heaters performance, compares it to the desired values (called the setpoints), and adjusts the fuel and oxygen flow rates to minimize the differences. For example, if the heater's operating temperature is not as high as called for by the central computer, more fuel and/or oxygen are needed. However, the ratio of the two must be maintained properly so that pollution requirements are not exceeded or fuel efficiency is not degraded. In order to optimize all the factors, the microprocessor will have to do numerous calculations and make many decisions based on the data it has been given. See Figure 3.2.

The software programs used to control this system will require appreciable time and effort to write but will require even more time to test and find all the faults. This latter process is called debugging. It includes not only finding the mistakes in the purely software routines but in those that control the hardware and in the hardware operation as well. Also, the system operation (the combination of hardware and software) must

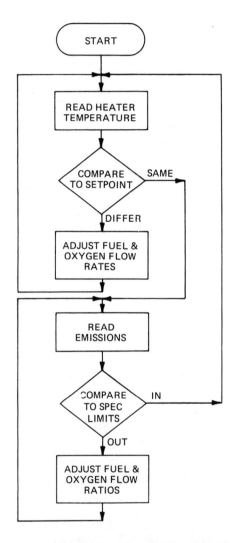

Figure 3.2 Heater Control System Control Program

be tested to ensure that the control is stable and reliable. Software/hardware trade-offs may have to be made during design for optimum speed, or safety, or to minimize software complexity. These subjects will be covered in the following chapters. The software *flow-charts* developed for this system are shown in Appendix A.

Since the primary objective of this book is to explain hardware/software debugging techniques, a number of design choices will be made that will better illustrate some of the debugging methods as opposed to design techniques. For example, there are a number of ways that the fuel/oxygen flow rate can be monitored and controlled. One method uses flow meters in the fuel/oxygen lines with output pulse rates which are proportional to the flow. These pulses can be connected to a programmable counter/timer, that can convert the pulse rate to a digital representation of the fuel/oxygen flow. This information can then be used by the microcomputer to control the position of the valves to adjust the flow to an optimum value. Another method uses an instrumented valve that has a known flow rate as a function of its determined position (the fuel pressure would have to be known or constant). The microcomputer can then read the position of the valve, compare it to the prescribed position or flow rate and adjust the position of the valve accordingly. In this example system a flow meter will be used to monitor flow rates.

To select the complement of microcomputer hardware required, all of the control system's input and output signal requirements must be defined. Since this is a digital system, it is desirable to select external equipment so that each line will be controllable with TTL level signals which are either HIGH or LOW. If this is not possible or cost effective, then equipment within the microcomputer will be required to convert the signals to digital. In this Plant Heater Control System example, the input and output wiring requirements and signals for each peripheral device are:

1. Fuel and Oxygen Control Valves:
   Two electrically controlled valves will be used to adjust the fuel and oxygen flow rates. Since this is a new system design, valve controllers will be selected that use standard TTL signal levels. The required TTL signals for each valve are as follows:

   A. RUN/STOP control – HIGH (1) = RUN
   　　　　　　　　　　　 – LOW (0) = STOP

   B. Direction control　 – HIGH (1) = Clockwise
   　　　　　　　　　　　 – LOW (0) = Counter-
   　　　　　　　　　　　　　　　　　　clockwise

2. Fuel and Oxygen Flow Rate Meters:
   Two in-line flow rate meters will be used to monitor the fuel and oxygen. Meters will be selected that output TTL level pulses at a rate proportional to the actual flow rates.

3. Exhaust Gas Monitor:
   A gas analyzer will be used to monitor the flue gas for excess oxygen and unburned combustibles. An instrument will be selected that will output its data, whenever the microcomputer requests it, as two se-

quential 8-bit data bytes, with each byte accompanied by a TTL level *Data Available* signal. *The Data Request* signal will also be a TTL level signal.

The following devices do not provide digital TTL signals:

4. Heater Temperature Monitor:
   A type B thermocouple will be used to monitor the heater temperature. This thermocouple generates a low-level (millivolt) analog signal proportional to the heater temperature. This signal will need to be converted to a digital value for use by the microcomputer.

5. Supervisory Computer Interface:
   A data communications link is required between the Heater Control System that we are describing, and the Main Plant Supervisory Computer. This function is typically handled by a standard serial input/output *port* on the microcomputer system that has been implemented with an Asynchronous Communications Interface Adapter (ACIA) or equivalent. This port's external signal levels are not TTL but are provided by a built-in *RS232C* standard interface. We will not dwell on this since it has little to do with the subjects we are covering.

6. Operator Console Interface:
   An Operators Console for local on-site monitoring and control of the Heater System will be provided by a panel mounted keyboard and display. This terminal will interface to the Heater Control System

through the same type of serial interface as previously described.

A Summary of these Input/Output signal lines is shown in Table 3.1 and Figure 3.3.

HARDWARE IMPLEMENTATION

The decision was made to design this system with standard off-the-shelf modules. In order to provide useful and practical design information, a number of specific details are given. For

TABLE 3.1
Input/Output Wiring Requirements

Function	TTL Output	TTL Input	Analog Input	Serial I/O
Valve Control	4			
Flow Meter		2 pulses		
Gas Analyzer	1	8 data		
		1 control		
Temperature			2	
Supervisory				1-RS232C
Op. Console				1-RS232C
Totals	5	11	2	24 lines

1. The two serial ports use an RS232C interface. This is an *EIA* standard which defines the signal levels as well as the mechanical connections. Up to 12 wires are required.

2. The analog inputs require shielded twisted pair lines because of the low signal levels.

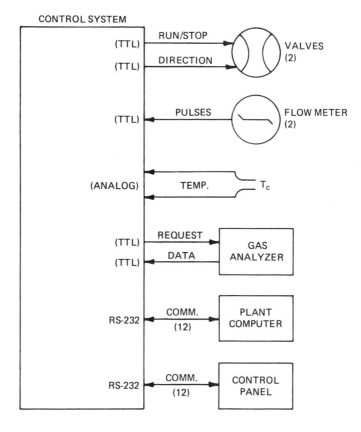

Figure 3.3 Control System Interfaces

those readers who are not concerned with the design details at this time, a cursory over view may be in order. The following complement of Motorola Micromodules will be used:

1. Microcomputer Module—M68MM17. (see Figure 3.4) This Single-Board Computer (SBC) provides many of the required input/output interfaces. It uses the 6809 microprocessor with a *crystal controlled clock oscillator* and has provisions for 2048 bytes of

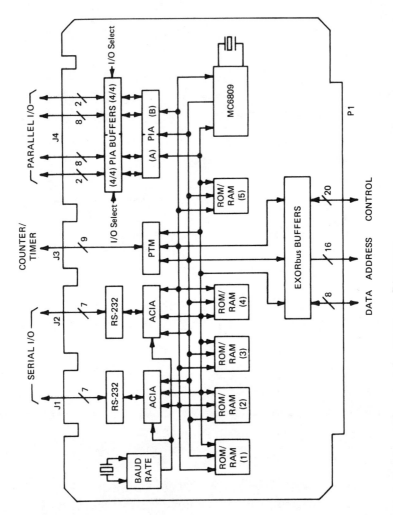

Figure 3.4 Micromodule 17 Block Diagram

RAM and up to 32K bytes of ROM or EPROM for program control. Two parallel eight-bit input or output data ports with their associated *handshake* control lines, two asynchronous serial data ports with RS-232C interface and a triple 16-bit Programmable Timer (PTM) are also included.

The microprocessor's address, data and control lines are *buffered* and brought out to an *edge connector* so that additional input/output and memory modules can be added to the system through an interconnecting bus motherboard. This one module meets all of the system input/output requirements except for the low level analog signal.

2. Analog-to-Digital (A/D) Converter Module — M68MM15B. (see Figure 3.5). As previously indicated, the interface with the low-level thermocouple signal presents three problems that must be resolved. When the thermocouple leads (platinum/rhodium in the case of a type B thermocouple) are connected to the A/D input, a secondary thermocouple effect is generated. This potential error is compensated for on this module by a cold-junction compensation circuit. Also, the voltage out of a thermocouple is non-linear. This A/D converter module, when commanded by the microprocessor, will convert the input analog low-level voltage into a linear 15-bit (plus sign) digital representation of the temperature in degrees C. At the end of conversion the module will interrupt the processor so that it can then read the data.

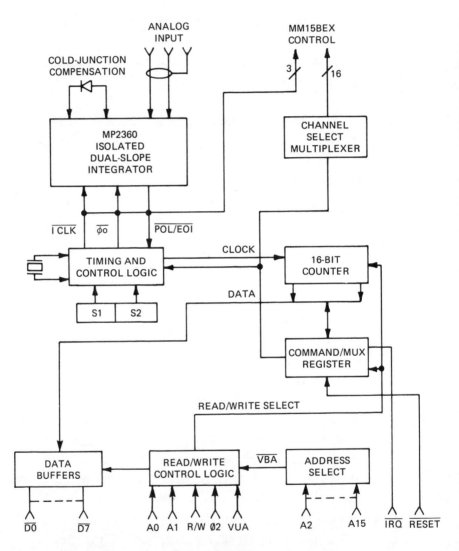

Figure 3.5 Micromodule M68MM15B Block Diagram

3. System Packaging and Control Panel—M68MMSC1. Since this system requires only two modules,they can be housed in a *Chassis* which includes a five-slot card cage, a motherboard, and a power supply. This supply provides the required $+5$, $+12$, and -12 VDC operating voltages. It is a rack mountable chassis with cooling fan.

4. The Operator Console function will be provided by a Burr-Brown Model TM71-IO Microterminal which provides a full alpha/numeric keyboard and 16-character display. It also has eight user-defined function keys and function lights. It interfaces to the microcomputer through an RS-232C serial link.

The overall results of the preceding description can best be seen in the Functional Block Diagram of the Control System, Figure 3.6.

SIGNAL ASSIGNMENTS

Now that the general hardware requirements have been defined it is necessary to assign specific input/output signals to specific input/output functions on the microcomputer modules.

1. Valve Control Signal:
Each of the two valves require two TTL level input control signals, RUN/STOP and CW/CCW direction. The parallel port on the microcomputer module is implemented with a Peripheral Interface Adapter

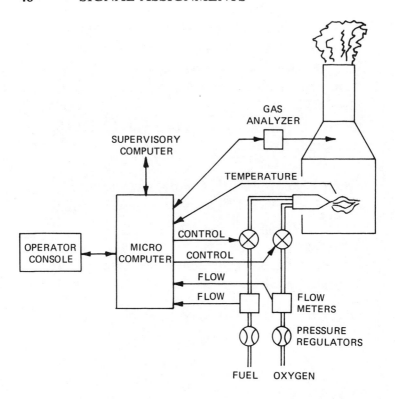

Figure 3.6 Plant Boiler Monitor and Control System

(PIA). This programmable parallel I/O device has two separate eight-bit data ports that can be programmed to be either input or output signal lines. Two of these data lines on the **B** half of the device will be used to control the oxygen valve and two to control the fuel valve as shown in Figure 3.7. Mnemonics will be assigned to each of these signals to aid in their identification when writing the software, as in Table 3.2. The remaining four data bits and the two control lines on the **B** side of the PIA are not used.

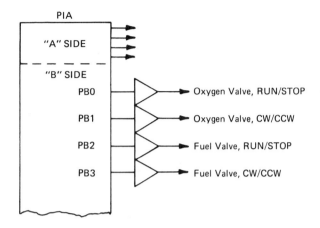

Figure 3.7 Valve Control Diagram

2. Gas Analyzer Signals:
   The Gas Analyzer monitors the flue gas for excess oxygen and unburned combustibles. The amounts of each are coded into two eight-bit words which are brought into the computer when the analyzer receives a TTL level Data Request signal. The presence of each of the two data words is indicated by a Data Available signal. This data transfer handshake mode

TABLE 3.2
Valve Control Bit Assignments

Mnemonic	PIA Bit	Function
OVR	PB0	One (High) = RUN, zero (low) = STOP
OVD	PB1	One (High) = CW, zero (low) = CCW
FVR	PB2	One (High) = RUN, zero (low) = STOP
FVD	PB3	One (High) = CW, zero (low) = CCW

of operation is directly compatible with the operation of the remaining half of the PIA as shown in Figure 3.8. The mnemonics, associated signals, and functions are as in Table 3.3. The configuring of the PIA to operate in these various modes will be discussed later in the software section.

3. Flow Meter Signals:

The flow meters in line with the oxygen and fuel lines output a TTL level pulse train. The frequency of the pulses is proportional to the rate of flow of the oxygen and fuel into the furnace burner. The microcomputer module has a Programmable Timer Module (PTM) function which provides three 16-bit counter/timers. The output pulses from the two flow meters will each be connected to the input of one of the PTM counters. The third counter will be used to pro-

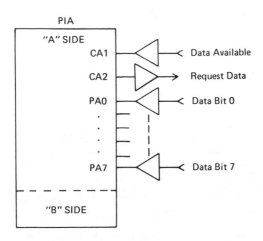

Figure 3.8 Gas Analyzer Diagram

TABLE 3.3
Gas Analyzer Bit Assignments

Mnemonics	PIA Bit	Function
GAD0	PA0	Gas Analyzer data bit zero
|	|	
GAD7	PA7	Gas Analyzer data bit seven
GADR	CA2	Gas Analyzer data request
GADA	CA1	Gas Analyzer data available

vide a time base for counting the flow meter pulses (see Figure 3.9).

4. Thermocouple Analog Signal:
   The two output leads from the thermocouple are connected to the input connector on the A/D converter module (see Figure 3.10). The module will be manually configured for a Type B thermocouple, and the operating mode of the A/D converter will be established in the initialization software for the system.

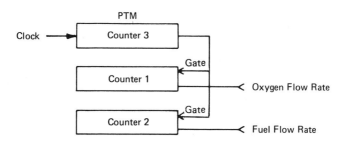

Figure 3.9 Flow Meter Diagram

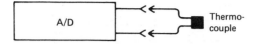

Figure 3.10 Thermocouple Diagram

5. Serial Communication Signals:
The microcomputer module provides two asynchronous serial communication ports with RS-232C interfaces. The required transmission speed or *baud rate* for the two channels (supervisory computer and operator's console), will be manually configured on the board. The mode of operation of the two Asynchronous Communication Interface Adapters (ACIAs) will also be established during initialization by the software (see Figure 3.11).

With the completion of the assignments of specific microcomputer input/output signals to their system functions, it is now time to consider the software requirements.

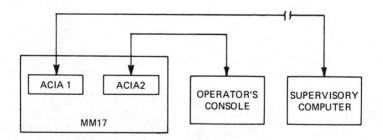

Figure 3.11 Communication Diagram

SOFTWARE
REQUIREMENTS

One of the initial design activities is to *flow-chart* the required software. The flow chart for this application example is shown in Figure 3.12.

Note that only major software modules are shown in this diagram. Detailed flow charts for each module will be developed in later chapters.

A description of the function of each software module follows:

RESET — Whenever power is initially applied to the system, the microcomputer module generates a system RESET signal. It also has a switch that can be used by the operator to reset the system. In this system the RESET signal resets the PIA parallel I/O device and the PTM timer/counter device on the microcomputer module as well as the A/D converter. At the end of the RESET pulse the 6809 microprocessor automatically reads the top two memory locations (called the RESET vector), and starts executing the program at that address. The designer's program must properly place the beginning address of the software *initialization* routines at the RESET vector location.

INITIALIZATION — This software module contains the sequence of instructions that configure the system for its required mode of operation. In this example the initialization code will:

1. Configure the two ACIAs so that communications

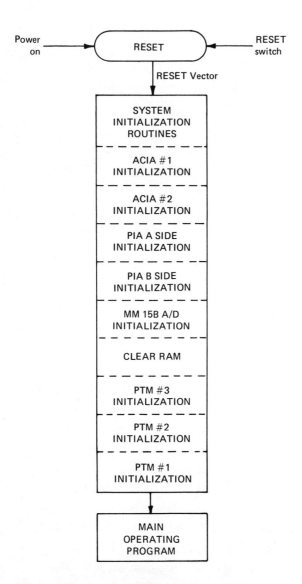

Figure 3.12 System Software Flow Chart

can be established with the Plant Supervisory computer and the Operator's console.

2. Configure the PIA so it can control the valves and
also receive data from the Gas Analyzer.

3. Configure the PTM so two of the channels can monitor the output of the flow meters and the third channel generates a time base.

4. Configure the A/D converter module so it can properly monitor the output of the heater thermocouple.

5. Clear (make all zeros) a section of RAM that will
be used to store system operating parameters.

Once the initialization is complete the controlled operation of
the system can begin.

MAIN OPERATING
PROGRAM

This program contains a number of sub-modules as shown in
Figure 3.13, and described as follows:

Setpoint Temperature — When the heater subsystem has been
reset, it alerts the Main Plant Supervisory Computer. The desired setpoint temperature is then transmitted to the control
system. This value is stored in RAM and used by the subsystem to control the heater.

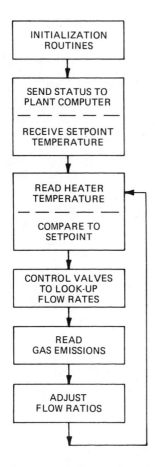

Figure 3.13 Main Operating Program Flow Chart

Read Heater Temperature — Once the desired setpoint temperature is received and stored, the control system can then read the heater temperature from the A/D converter. A software routine may be required to convert the A/D data to the same format as the data received from the Plant Supervisory Computer.

Compare Temperatures — Now that the control system has both the setpoint temperature and the actual heater temperature, they can be compared so that a decision can be made as to how to control the fuel/oxygen flow rates.

Adjust Fuel/Oxygen Flow Rates — Based on the results of the temperature comparison, a *look-up table* can be accessed to determine the initial oxygen and fuel flow rates that are required to adjust the heater temperatures to match the setpoint temperature. The flow rates can be read and the valves can be adjusted until the actual flow rates match the required flow rates. However, since this control system is also required to maximize the fuel efficiency and minimize the pollutant emissions, the control system must request data from the Gas Analyzer and use this information to adjust the ratio between the fuel and oxygen.

Not only is the adjustment of the fuel and oxygen an iterative process but the control system must continually monitor everything so that changes in the setpoint temperature generated by the Plant Supervisory Computer or changes in the heater performance can be accomodated.

This completes the software design goals and thus, the system design. Obviously, the system designer could at this point, configure the hardware, generate the complete system software, connect the control system to the plant heater, and then start trying to test or debug everything. Just as obviously, this is not the way to do it. A step-at-a-time, organized approach should be used to test the pieces individually, and then as a system. This is the rest of the story and will be described in the following chapters.

CHAPTER 4
PROCEDURE FOR
DEVELOPMENT—
HARDWARE EMULATION

There are almost as many ways to approach a system development as there are engineers, so it is difficult to suggest a best way. Many engineers will want to build a part of the system, test it, add another part, test it, and continue this iterative process until the system is complete. This is also a good way for microcomputer system designers to begin.

MICROCOMPUTER DEVELOPMENT SYSTEMS

Microcomputer Development Systems (MDSs), such as Motorola's EXORciser, are designed to make the engineers job easier. Many features are included which reduce the time required to develop and prototype a working model. The 6809 version of the EXORciser can be used with any 6809 based system, but Micromodules in general have special features which simplify their use with the EXORciser for system hardware and software development.

The EXORciser includes a microprocessor module and a debug module which make up the debug system (see Figure 4.1). Other memory or I/O modules can be added as appropriate. When equipped with a disk and a printer (by installing a *Floppy Disk Controller* and Printer Interface module), the EXORciser serves as the software development station. In addition however, the EXORciser has several other important applications. One is to allow the quick assembly of modules with which to *emulate* the proposed system, or part of it, for testing.

The EXORciser closely duplicates the final system in performance and thus any software tested in the EXORciser will work properly in the final user's system. A second purpose is to debug the entire prototype system including the external hardware. The EXORciser is especially useful in evaluating the hardware/software interfaces. For this purpose the features built into the debug module are used. This module

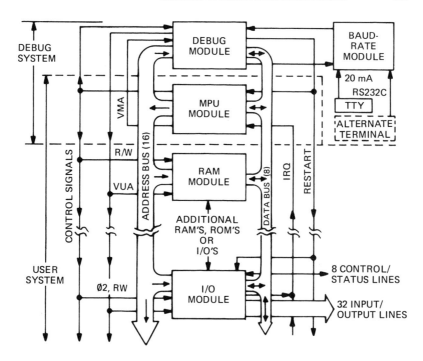

Figure 4.1 EXORciser Simplified Block Diagram

includes a *monitor program* ROM called EXbug, which makes the EXORciser an intelligent instrument. Several unique hardware circuits are also provided on the debug module to aid debugging. Three of them are the ABORT, Run-One-Instruction, and Stop-On-Address circuits. Use of these features will be described in later chapters.

The EXORciser uses a standard RS-232C *ASCII* terminal as a means for the engineer to communicate with the system. It can be any CRT terminal, a TI silent 700, or even a teletypewriter. If the terminal uses paper it can eliminate the need for the printer but is very much slower. The TI terminal and the teletypewriter have tape facilities for loading or storing programs but a Floppy Disk System, a CRT, and a Printer are often used because of their speed. This results in a decrease in development time.

Developing a self-regulating microcomputer control system, or any microcomputer system, usually must begin by determining how to control the external hardware (the valves in this case) and, for this system, how to sense the heater performance. That is, the input/output interface should be developed first. This will allow the software and its logic to be planned. The system to be built was described in the previous chapter and shown in Figure 3.1. To exactly emulate the I/O of the final system, the single board computer module, Micromodule 17 (MM17) in this case, is installed in the EXORciser. Because MM17 includes a 6809 microprocessor, the EXORciser MPU module is not needed. The testing configuration planned is shown in Figure 4.2.

It includes the entire final system, plus the EXORciser modules needed to do the testing and develop the software. The EXORciser RAM modules are used to hold the initial versions of the system software so that they can be debugged or easily corrected. This application program will ultimately be located in EPROMs or ROMs on MM17. When the system has been debugged and is operational, with the software in RAM, the user's program can be reassembled at the addresses required to match the MM17 memory socket addresses. It can then be programmed into EPROMs (using a PROM programmer) and

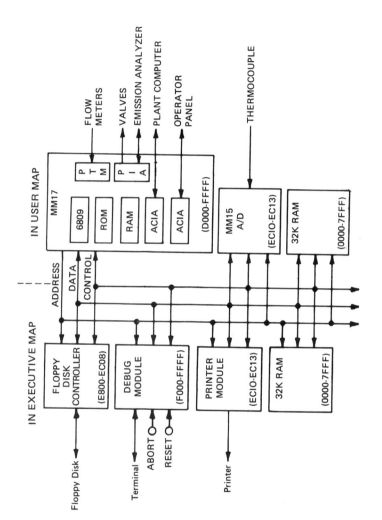

Figure 4.2 System Emulation in the EXORciser

installed in MM17 for final testing before the emulated system is removed from the EXORciser.

DEVELOPMENT
SYSTEM
MEMORY MAPPING

Figure 4.3 depicts the total memory that a 6809 microprocessor can address with its 16 address lines. This *memory map*, as it's called, is shown divided into blocks of 400 hexadecimal (1024 decimal) locations. Most memory ICs or assemblies are multiples of 1024. The scheme used when dealing with hexadecimal addresses is shown. The full map has sixty four blocks for a total of 65536 locations. In the EXORciser, the top four blocks are used by the EXbug program.

Figure 4.4 shows two such maps, and for the moment let's say the left one (called *Executive Map*) is the EXORciser Development System's map. In addition to EXbug, much of the memory space in this map is used by the disk controller and RAM modules needed for the Motorola Disk Operating System (MDOS). The *User Map*, on the right in Figure 4.4, shows the normal locations of the devices on MM17, and a suggested location for the registers of MM15B. If the EXORciser and User systems were to be placed in the same map, there would be some overlapping. It is possible to relocate some of the devices, on MM17 to avoid this, but it is rather complicated. Fortunately, EXORciser II has the capability to address two separate maps and avoid the difficulty. The EXbug program has two commands (EXEC and USER) which are used to select the de-

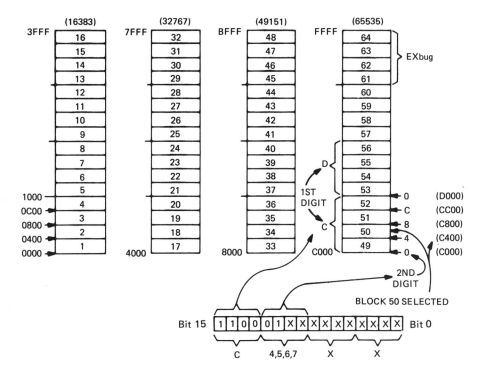

Figure 4.3 16 Bit Memory Map Showing Address Selection

ɔired map. The printer and disk interface modules operate in the Executive map along with EXbug, and the user's system devices (on MM17 and MM15B in this case) can occupy all or part of the USER map. One RAM module is needed in the Executive map to run the disk system and another is needed in the User map to hold the user's programs while they are under development. The modules are assigned to the appropriate map as shown in Figures 4.2 and 4.4 by proper installation of the Valid eXecutive Address (VXA) or Valid User Address (VUA) jumpers.

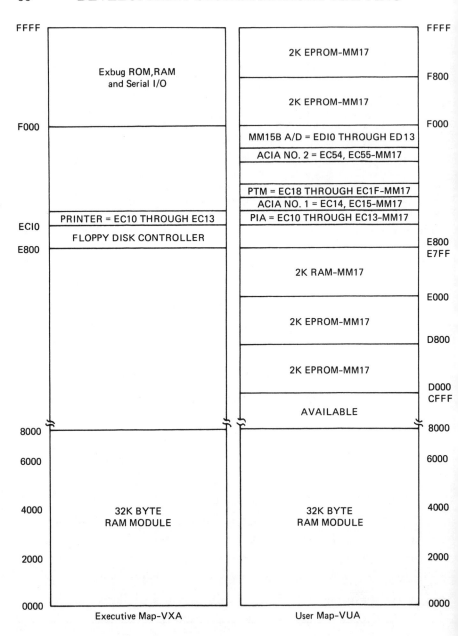

Figure 4.4 EXORciser Dual Memory Map

DEVELOPMENT
PROCEDURES

As shown in Figure 4.5, the procedure for designing and verifying a microcomputer system usually follows two parallel paths; one for hardware and one for software. Also, however, we will divide the process of development into phases, as follows:

1. Evaluating I/O hardware interfaces.

2. Development and testing of I/O software routines.

3. Development and testing of system modular routines.

4. Development and testing of the total program (and hardware).

All of the above will normally be done with the:

1. Micromodules in the EXORciser.

2. Programs in RAM.

3. System interfaces simulated.

4. Work being done in the laboratory.

For initial development, the system hardware (Valves, Flow Meters, Thermocouple, and Gas Analyzer) can probably be placed on the lab bench and electrically connected. Steps 1 and 2 must be done for each of the subsystems before steps 3 and 4 can be started. In fact, 3 and 4 can not really be final-

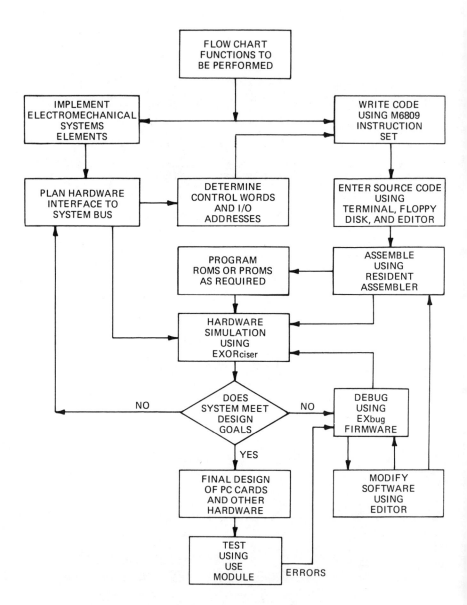

Figure 4.5 System Designing and Verifying Procedure

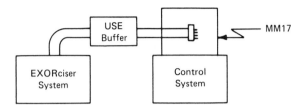

Figure 4.6 Testing with USE

ized until the system is moved to the plant environment and the I/O is completely operational. The program development can all be done with the program in the EXORciser's RAM (loaded and saved by means of the disk operating system).

When reasonably sure that the *bugs* are out, the program can be reassembled at the correct addresses and put into EPROMs. At some point in the development, it will be necessary to connect the test system to the plant interface in order to properly check the hardware/software interactions. This can be done in several ways. The EXORciser and Disk system can be placed on a cart or the equipment relocated to a bench at the plant control site. With the cables connected to the installed hardware, testing can be continued with the subsystems in partial operation. This can continue until the final EPROMs are installed and tested with the Micromodules still in the EXORciser. The modules could then be moved to their own chassis and the final tests repeated. This completes the job. Alternatively, the Micromodules can be moved to their own chassis in the lab or in the plant, and connected to the EXORciser by means of the Users System Evaluator (USE). See Figure 4.6. This is an accessory item that allows the EXORciser to be connected into any 6809 system by plugging in the USE cable in place of the 6809 chip. When connected in this way, the user's system can be in its final configuration, and yet the full debugging capability of the EXORciser is available for final system debugging. When using USE, the program can still reside in EXORciser RAM. Run-One-Instruction, ABORT, and Halt-On-Address functions can also be used with the program in EPROM.

HARDWARE EMULATION

Once we understand these overall goals and have configured the EXORciser, we can proceed with the hardware emulation. We will assume that the first step is to analyze the valve subsystem hardware interface. To do so, the valves (on the bench) are connected as shown in Figure 4.2. The next step is to determine the PIA programming required to send commands to the external valve hardware. The PIA has 16 lines (or pins) which can be programmed as inputs or outputs. They are normally treated as two 8-bit ports. However, on MM17, these PIA data lines are buffered with high current IC drivers, in groups of four. See Figure 3.4. The buffers must be selected to be incoming or outgoing by means of jumpers. There are also two handshake lines associated with each 8-bit port. The two ports are normally referred to as the **A** side and the **B** side of the PIA.

VALVE CONTROL

In Chapter 3 it was decided to use the first four lines of the **B** side of the PIA to control the operation of the valves (see Table 3-2). The remaining four data lines and two control lines are unused. In order to use these lines as outputs, the proper jumper must be installed on MM17 to select the buffer direction. Also, after installing MM17 in the EXORciser and connecting it to the valves, the PIA must be programmed so that the associated data lines behave as outputs. Three internal 8-bit registers are associated with each side of the PIA as depicted in Figure 4.7. Either the **B** side Data or Direction register is accessed at address $EC12, depending on the state of bit 2 of the Control/Status register. The Control/Status register (at $EC13) is a single register with two read only status bits (bits 6 and 7), five control bits (bits 0, 1, 3, 4, and 5) to select the PIA modes, and bit 2 (the Data/Direction register switch).

The **B** Control/Status register is normally programmed to:

1. Control the mode of operation for the CB1 line on the **B** side by the state of bits 0 and 1.

2. Control the mode for the CB2 line by the state of bits 3, 4, and 5.

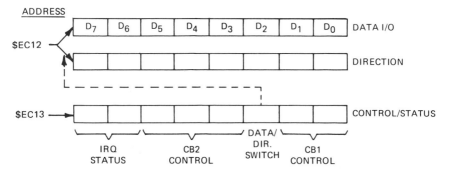

Figure 4.7 PIA Internal Registers

3. Control whether the Direction or Data register is accessed depending on the state of bit 2.

4. Indicate whether CB1 has signalled an interrupt (bit 7).

5. Indicate whether CB2 has signalled an interrupt (bit 6).

Because we do not use either CB1 or CB2 in this application, it would appear the only bit we are concerned with is bit 2. However, since these lines are capable of causing *interrupts* we should make certain they do not. This can be done by programming them properly. On MM17, both lines are connected to pullup resistors, so they will remain HIGH. When the system is first turned on, the RESET line will clear all registers which selects the Direction register and causes the data lines to be selected as inputs. We must therefore, write all ones ($0F or %00001111) to the four *Least Significant Bits* (LSBs) of the direction register (at $EC12) to make the lines appear as outputs. Then we need to write a 1 to bit 2 (04 or %00000100) of the Control/Status register at $EC13 to switch out the direction register and make the data register accessible at $EC12). In addition, it will be seen by referring to the PIA Data Sheet, that the CB1 and CB2 lines have been programmed by the 0s in the control word to modes which are harmless. Since these PIA registers appear in the memory map just the same as memory, the Display/Change Memory routine of EXbug is used to read or write to them for test purposes. This technique is very helpful to verify the electrical interface and to learn of any hardware limitations before attempting to write any software. This process of manually programming the PIA has been described so we can now proceed to test the valve electrical interface operation.

Recall that we have selected valves that can be opened or closed with TTL level signals (see Table 3.2). They can therefore be directly connected to the buffered PIA outputs on the SBC (MM17). One line selects the direction (opening or closing), and the other causes the motor to run, to actually move the valve.

Figure 4.8 shows the PIA data register bit assignments to control the valves (from Table 3.2). If we were to use the Memory Display/Change routine of EXbug to write a 03 (00000011) into the data register, the oxygen valve should run clockwise. Before doing this, however, it would be wise to have a switch set up to remove power from the valve when desired. If a 00 is written quickly enough, that might not be necessary. Similarly, writing a $0C (00001100) should move the fuel valve

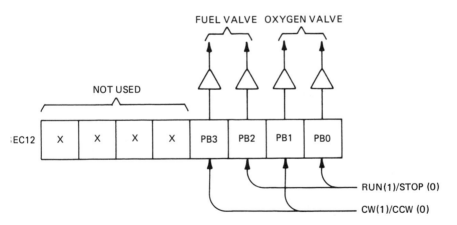

Figure 4.8 PIA B-Side Data Register Bit Assignment

clockwise. Since the **1s** of the command word (8-bits of data) cause the associated output pins of the PIA to go to a TTL HIGH level (2.0 to 5.25 volts, and the **0s** result in a LOW level (0 to 0.8 volts) on the other pins, a scope or voltmeter can be used to verify whether the proper signals are on the valve control lines as expected. If they are not, the wires can be moved to the proper pins or the command word can be verified.

The purpose of this analysis of the hardware interface is threefold:

1. To find the appropriate programming or control bytes to initialize the PIA for proper interfacing with the external valve hardware.

2. To verify the command byte written to the data register for activating the external valves.

3. To understand the hardware limitations when writing the control software.

Once these bytes have been determined, they will be used, as shown in the "System Designing and Verifying Procedure" of Figure 4.5, to develop the I/O software routines or I/O *drivers*. These drivers will be used by the Application system logic programs to control the hardware. Similar I/O routines are needed for each of the subsystems (i.e., Valve control, Flow Meter sensing, Temperature sensing, and the Gas Analyzer readings).

Normally, after the hardware analysis of the valve subsystem has been done, an engineer would proceed to write the I/O drivers for this subsystem, and to do so he or she should study the following chapters to learn techniques for software development. However, when the valve subsystem is operational, the hardware for the next subsystem needs to be evaluated. An alternate procedure would be to continue the hardware testing of all subsystems before proceeding to the software development. We will, therefore, describe the other subsystems.

FLOW METER MONITORING

The Flow Meter subsystem is the one to naturally follow in the design plan. Testing the Flow Rate hardware and software will be more complex than the valve control portion that we just tested. The 6840 PTM is more difficult to set up properly and, at this state of development, we cannot use the Flow Meters to generate the TTL level inputs. Therefore, it is suggested that a laboratory pulse generator be used to simulate the PTM inputs. We will be using PTM counter 3 to generate a fixed gate signal for counters 1 and 2 and they will count the Flow Meter signals as shown in Figure 4.9a.

We can test the operation of counter 3 as follows:

1. Reference to the 6840 data sheet will show that by writing an 10000101 ($85) pattern into the control register, we have programmed counter 3 to:

    A. Divide by 8

    B. Use external clock

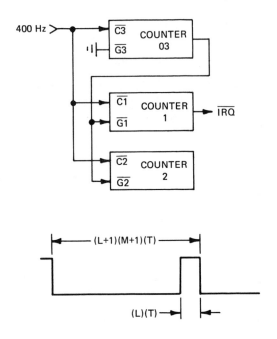

Figure 4.9a Interconnections of Counters in PTM

Figure 4.9b Timing of Counter 3

C. Use continuous dual 8-bit mode

D. Mask interrupt

E. Enable output

The PTM control register of MM17 is located at address $EC18.

1. If we use a 400 Hz square wave to pulse the clock input of counter 3 then the output clock period, after the divide by 8, will be 20 ms. To generate a 10 second sample period will then require 500 of these 20

ms clocks pulses. Again, reference to the 6840 data sheet will show that we can generate a 10 second gate signal (LOW) with a 20 ms off period (HIGH) as follows (see Figure 4.9b):

A. The timing formula for the continuous dual 8-bit mode is **(L) (t)** for the off period and **(L + 1) (M + 1) (t)** for the full cycle period. L is the number to be loaded in the least significant byte of the counter latch and **M** is the number loaded in the most significant byte. **t** is the time period of the input clock, in this case, 20 ms. Therefore, for a minimum off period of 20 ms the value of **L** is 1. The formula for the ON period (10 sec) is **[M(L + 1) + 1] [t]** = 10 seconds. Since **L** = 1 and **t** = 20 ms, then **M** = 250, which will result in an actual ON period of 10.02 seconds.

B. The values to be loaded into the counter 3 latches will then be **M** = 250 = 11111010 = $FA and **L** = 1 = 00000001 = $01. Therefore the number $FA01 is to be loaded into addresses $EC1E and $EC1F.

3. The same 400 Hz signal can be used to simulate the flow meter inputs to counters 1 and 2. Reference to the 6840 data sheet will show that we can operate these two counters in the pulse width comparison mode to count the number of input signals during the 10.02 second gate period. One of the counters (number 1) can be programmed to generate an interrupt when the gate signal goes high, at the end of

the gate period. This will signal the processor that a flow rate count is available in both counter 1 and 2. To configure counter 1 to the external clock, 16-bit count, pulse width comparison, output disabled and IRQ enabled modes, we need to write 01011000 ($58) into control register 1 at $EC18. To configure counter 2 to the same modes except for disabling the IRQ we need to write a 00011001 ($19) into Control Register 2 at $EC19.

4. To set up the 6840 hardware on MM17 we need to connect the output of counter 3 to the gate inputs of counters 1 and 2. This can be accomplished by jumpers on the MM17 module. The 400 Hz input can be connected to the PTM input connector on MM17.

5. Because of the nature of the operation of the PTM we will need to program it, using the Memory Display/Change Routine, in the following sequence:

A. Write counter 3 latches with $FA at $EC1E and $01 at $EC1F.

B. Write Control Register 3 with $85 at $EC18.

C. Write Control Register 2 with $19 at $EC19.

D. Write Control Register 1 with $58 at $EC18, (Note that when Control Register 2 has a 1 in bit position 0 the PTM allows access to Control Reg-

ister 1 which is at the same address as Control
Register 3.)

E. When a **0** is written into bit position 7 of Control Register 1 the counters will start to operate.
When the interrupt occurs after 10 seconds, both
counters 1 and 2 should have been decremented
from their initial value of 65,536 ($FFFF) by
4000 (+ or − 1 count). The code that should be
in the counters is therefore $FFFF − $0FA3 or,
$F05C with an allowance for the stability of the
input signal generator.

To clear the interrupt, it is necessary to read the Status
Register at $EC19, the counter 1 Data Register at $EC1A, and
the counter 2 Data Register at $EC1B. These reads must be per-
formed during the 20 ms off-time in order to keep the operation in synchronism. Therefore, an interrupt service routine
must be used to read the Status Register and the four data registers. Figure 4.10 shows such an IRQ service routine.

ANALOG INPUT
MONITORING

The Temperature subsystem, which uses the A/D converter
module (MM15B), is the next to be examined. The module must
first be configured, through the use of the on-board jumpers,
for the type of thermocouple to be used and to establish the
module's base address for its registers. The module is then in-

```
 1 P                           NAM  FLOW
 2 P                 *    Program to Initialize and Test
 3 P                 *       The Flow Meter PTM
 4 A        EC18     PTMCRS  EQU       $EC18         Control Reg1/3 Select
 5 A        EC19     PTMCR2  EQU       $EC19         Control Reg2/Status
 6 A        EC1A     PTMTC1  EQU       $EC1A         MSB Buffer/Time1
 7 A        EC1B     PTMTL1  EQU       $EC1B         Latch1/LSB Buffer
 8 A        EC1C     PTMTC2  EQU       $EC1C         MSB Buffer/Time2
 9 A        EC1D     PTMTL2  EQU       $EC1D         Latch2/LSB Buffer
10 A        EC1E     PTMTC3  EQU       $EC1E         MSB Buffer/Time3
11 A        EC1F     PTMTL3  EQU       $EC1F         Latch3/LSB Buffer
12 A        F564     PIAIRQ  EQU       $F564         Return To EXbug
13 P                 *
14 A        3200              ORG      $3200
15 A 3200 0002       OXYFLO  RMB       2             Oxygen Flow Data
16 A 3202 0002       FULFLO  RMB       2             Fuel Flow Data
17 A                 *
18 A                 * PTM Initialization (See Chapter 4, Fig. 4.9)
19 A                 *
20 A 3204 8685       PTMINIT LDA       #%10000101
21 A 3206 B7EC18             STA       PTMCRS        Set Counter 3 Mode
22 A 3209 FCFAD1             LDD       $FAD1
23 A 320C FDEC1E             STD       PTMTC3        Load Counter 3 M & L
24 A 320F 8619              LDA       #%00011001
25 A 3211 B7EC19             STA       PTMCR2        Set Counter 2 Mode
26 A 3214 8658              LDA       #%01011000
27 A 3216 B7EC18             STA       PTMCRS        Set Cntr 1 Mode, Start
28 A 3219 39                RTS
29 A                 *
30 A                 * PTMIRQ Routine (See Chapter 4, Fig. 4.10).
31 A                 *
32 A 321A B6EC19     PTMIRQ  LDA       PTMCR2        Read Status Register
33 A 321D 2A45               BPL       PIAIRQ        Not PTM - Try PIA
34 A 321F FCEC1A             LDD       PTMTC1        Read Oxygen Flow Rate
35 A 3222 FD3200             STD       OXYFLO        Store Data
36 A 3225 FCEC1C             LDD       PTMTC2        Read Fuel Flow Data
37 A 3228 FD3202             STD       FULFLO        Store Data in RAM
38 A 322B 39                RTS
39 A                 *
                             END
```

Figure 4.10 PTM Initialization and Interrupt Service Routine

stalled in the EXORciser and the thermocouple lines connected. The registers can be manually programmed for testing by again using the Memory Display/Change routine for EXbug. As described in the MM15B manual, there are four registers starting at the base address just selected. The proposed control words are written into the first two locations and the data is read from the last two. When it is determined that the module is properly programmed and jumpered, the magnitude of the data will be related to the temperature at the thermocouple. Some known temperatures can be generated using a calibrating source and readings can be taken from the data registers. When sufficient data has been obtained to verify the temperature subsystems correct operation, the control word information is put aside until the software development is started.

**GAS ANALYZER
MONITORING**

The Gas Analyzer uses the **A** side of the PIA. In this case the eight data lines need to be programmed as inputs which is the direction established during reset. The CA1 and CA2 control lines will be used to handshake with the Gas Analyzer's logic. The CA2 line is programmed as an output and used to request new data from the Analyzer. CA1 is normally an input and is used to tell the microcomputer when data is available on the PIA's input lines. The Gas Analyzer normally only responds when interrogated but could be programmed to continuously monitor the emission status of the exhaust and send an alarm if excessive levels were seen. When it is ready with information, a positive-going TTL level signal is sent on CA1. The data is the amount of carbon dioxide and the percent of unburned oxygen. As each byte of data is accepted, a positive pulse is sent on the CA2 line to request new information. (Once the lines are connected, the Memory Display/Change routine of EXbug can be used to test all these functions and verify that the analyzer data can be read from the PIA **A** Data register.)

    In order to test this Gas Analyzer operation we must program the PIA **A** side as follows:

1. Data bits as inputs (this is the "as Reset" condition).

2. CA2 as an output that will generate a positive going signal. This can be established by setting the **A** side Control Register bits 4 and 5 to **1s** and using bit 3 to control the CA2 signal. When bit 3 = **1**, CA2 will go HIGH or when bit 3 = **0**, CA2 will be LOW.

3. CA1 as an input that will cause a system interrupt when the Gas Analyzer outputs a data available pulse. This can be established by programming the Control Register bit 0 to a **1**, which enables the interrupt, and bit 1 to a **1**, which will then cause an interrupt when an input signal goes high. This is all accomplished by using the Memory Display/Change routine to write a $36 (00110110) to address $EC11. To request data from the Gas Analyzer the Control Register data is changed to $3E (00111110), causing CA2 to go HIGH and then back to $36 to take it LOW. When the PIA-**A** side interrupt is generated by CA1 going high, the data can be read from address $EC10. Reading the data will clear the interrupt so that a second data byte can be detected by the next CA1 input.

SERIAL COMMUNICATIONS

The two serial communications ports on MM17 are used to communicate with the main plant computer and the operator control panel Microterminal. These ports use the M6850 Asynchronous Communications Interface Adapter (ACIA) devices and have RS-232C electrical signal interfaces. Jumpers on MM17 allow the two ports to be set up for proper use. In addition, the ACIAs must be configured by software to operate in the proper mode. The ACIAs each appear as two addressable memory locations whether reading or writing. There are actually four internal registers. The Status and Receive Data registers are read only. The Control and Transmit Data registers are write only.

On MM17 the two ACIA Control Registers are at addresses $EC14 (for ACIA No. 1) and $EC54 (for ACIA No. 2). The Control Registers must be programmed to configure the ACIAs for the required modes of operation. By referring to the 6850 Data Sheet, it will be seen that the ACIA does not have an external hardware reset function, and a *Master Reset* (03) pattern must first be written into control register bits CR0 and CR1. This can be done using the Display/Change routine of EXbug or by the initializing software routines to be described later. A second control word is then written to set the mode desired. This second word must first be determined by further reference to the Data Sheet with the following in mind.

For this application, we will specify that both the main plant computer and the Microterminal operate with 7 data bits, odd parity and one stop bit. It is suggested that an 8 section box be drawn like the one shown in Figure 4.11, and the bits entered as determined from the Data Sheet tables. The mode table will show that a 011 pattern should be used for bits CR4, CR3 and CR2. Control Register bits CR6 and CR5 should be a 01 pattern to take RTS low and enable the transmit interrupt. Bits CR1 and CR0 should 0 and 1, respectively, to provide "divide by 16" which is customarily used. CR7 should be

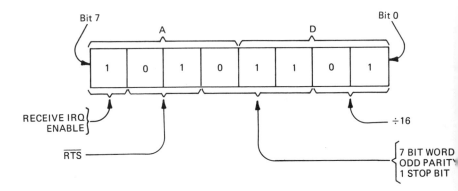

Figure 4.11 ACIA Control Register

a 1 to enable the receive interrupt. When these bits are all examined together it will be seen that the control word is $AD. This is then written to the Control Registers by the EXORciser Memory Display/Change routine.

The operation of the two serial ports can be tested on the bench by using the Microterminal. By attaching the Microterminal to serial port 1, with both the Microterminal and ACIA No. 1 set for the same baud rate, the Memory Display/ Change routine can be used to write a character to the ACIA Transmit Register at $EC15. For example, the character *A* would be $41. When that character is loaded into the ACIA Transmit Register it will automatically be sent to the Microterminal and displayed on the panel. Conversely, the character *A* key is pressed to transmit from the Microterminal to the ACIA, and the pattern $41 can be read from the Receive Register at $EC15. The Microterminal can also be used in the same way to test the other serial port.

The preceding paragraphs have described the evaluation of the hardware for each of the subsystems. The information gathered will be used in the following chapters to develop the various software modules needed for each of the subsystems. The debugging of them, as well as the overall system, will also be described.

CHAPTER 5
SOFTWARE
DEVELOPMENT
AND DEBUGGING

In Chapter 4 we used the EXORciser Display/Change memory routine to help us learn how to control the various Input/Output devices and to make sure they are operating properly with the hardware. We can now develop a sequence of instructions to write the control words, which were determined, to each of the Input/Output interface devices. This initialization routine must obviously be the first portion of code in our operational software.

**SOFTWARE
DEVELOPMENT**

There are many ways to produce the program. It could be written in a high-level language such as Pascal or Basic, or in 6809 *Assembly Language.* The techniques for debugging programs written in high level languages are different than those required for assembly language. There are advantages and disadvantages to both methods, and we will not attempt to present all the reasons for choosing either alternative. Some users believe that when interfacing to external hardware where a number of control lines must be manipulated, it is easier to use Assembly Language. The aspect of this approach which we feel is not fully understood is the debugging of the *machine code.* We will, therefore, concentrate on these techniques.

In order to use Assembly Language, it is advisable to study the Motorola 6809 Data Sheet and M6809PM(AD) Programming Manual prior to any software writing. If the original programming is done in a higher level language, the process called *compiling* will produce 6809 object (or machine) code modules. The compiler is never 100% efficient and frequently generates extra code. These additional instructions do not keep the program from running but occasionally take too much time or use too much memory space. Although not usually required, in cases where speed or size improvement is required, these modules can be dissassembled by using a program such as *SYMBUG09,* for analysis. Disassembly is the reverse process where machine language codes are translated into Assembly Language statements (mnemonics). Since the object codes are common to all methods of program generation and can be directly related to Assembly Language statements, we have chosen to use them in our examples.

The programs needed for this heater control application involve *bit manipulation* and with most high-level languages, this is not easily done. Assembly Language, on the other hand, does have many instructions that deal with individual bits. The AND or OR instructions, for example, can be used to RESET or SET any bit. This will be described later in this chapter. In fairness, we must point out that Assembly Language programming requires a more intimate knowledge of the microprocessor, particularly, of the register structure.

In Chapter 4 we described the use of a Microcomputer Development System (MDS) for analyzing the I/O circuits. As previously mentioned, these systems are also useful for software development. They allow the user to:

1. Type in the desired sequence of microprocessor instruction *mnemonics*, display them on the CRT terminal and then modify or *Edit* them until they appear to be correct. These Assembly Language statements are said to be mnemonic because they resemble the english words which describe their function and therefore make it easier for programmers to remember them. For example, the instruction **LDA #$E** means to **LoaD** the 6809 **A** register with the number (**#**) hexidecimal (**$**) **E**.

2. *Assemble* the object code; that is, to convert the Assembly Language instructions into machine codes. These are the binary bit patterns that the micro-

processor understands and uses to perform the requested instructions. These bits are assembled into bytes and assigned to sequential locations in memory. The instruction **LDA #$E** is translated to two bytes which are displayed in their hexidecimal form as **86 0E**. The **86** is the machine code equivalent of **LDA** and the **0E** is the value to be loaded into the **A** register.

3. *Link* and load the object code; that is, to link together the various object code modules for each function, into one contiguous file, and load it into RAM at the desired locations so that the program can be tested and debugged.

Note that during the assembly process, the assembler program will only accept valid mnemonics to be converted to machine language. If the user were to enter **LDE** for example, the assembler would print a *syntax error*. If, on the other hand a **LDD** was entered where **LDA** was intended, the assembler would generate code since this is an acceptable mnemonic. In this case, however the program would load the **D** register and improper operation would result when the program is executed. Both of these errors must be corrected by *editing* the Assembly Language *source* and reassembling it.

For this system application we will assume the program is written in assembly mnemonics using the Editor program, and the Assembler program is used to generate the Machine Code (object program), as well as the program *listing*. The program should be reedited and reassembled until it assembles without errors. This only means that the syntax for the chosen instructions is correct. Unfortunately, it does not mean the program will work properly when loaded into the development systems memory for testing. This is because the logic of the instructions is not verified by the assembler (or compiler, in the case of Pascal or Basic programs). This logic can only be verified by executing the program and this is why *system debugging* is needed. Debugging the system includes not only finding problems in the software, such as for calculations, but also verifying the software control of the hardware. The logical performance of the program must also be analyzed to determine whether the sequence of microcomputer instructions do what the programmer thinks they should. The failure to select the correct instructions in implementing logic is one of the principal reasons for errors.

COMPUTER DECISIONS

The logic that we are referring to is the way a computer makes a decision. In the case of the 6809 microprocessor, there are 16 of these decision-making instructions and they are known as *conditional branch instructions*. They are shown in Table 5.1.

Each of these instructions *tests* the status of bits in the *Condition Code Register* (CCR) of the 6809 (see Figure 5.1).

The bits of the CCR are SET (made equal to **1**) or RESET (made equal to 0) by the Arithmetic/Logic Unit (ALU) of the 6809, as each instruction is executed. For example, when a number is subtracted from another of equal value, the result

TABLE 5.1
MC6809 Branch Instructions

Instr.	Test	Description
BCS	$C = 1$	Branch if Carry Set
BCC	$C = 0$	Branch if Carry Clear
BEQ	$Z = 1$	Branch if EQual to zero
BNE	$Z = 0$	Branch if Not Equal to zero
BMI	$N = 1$	Branch if MInus
BPL	$N = 0$	Branch if PLus
BVC	$V = 0$	Branch if oVerflow is Clear (signed)
BVS	$V = 1$	Branch if oVerflow is Set (signed)
BHS	$C = 0$	Branch if Higher or the Same (unsigned)
BLO	$C = 1$	Branch if LOwer (unsigned)
BGE	$[N \oplus V] = 0$	Branch if Greater than or Equal to zero (signed)

is zero and the **Z** bit of the Condition Code Register (CCR) is SET **(= 1)**. Normally a program proceeds from instruction to instruction in sequence unless it encounters a jump **(JMP or JSR),** or a branch instruction. The branch instructions are either conditional (depending on the status bits) or unconditional. Several unconditional branches are listed at the bottom of Table 5.1. Probably the easiest way to understand conditional branch instructions is to examine the two instructions that *test*

TABLE 5.1 *(continued)*

Instr.	Test	Description
BLT	$[N \oplus V] = 1$	Branch if Less Than zero (signed)
BGT	$Z \bullet [N \oplus V] = 0$	Branch if Greater Than (signed)
BLE	$Z + [N \oplus V] = 1$	Branch if Less than or Equal to zero (signed)
BHI	$[C \oplus Z] = 0$	Branch if HIgher (un-signed)
BLS	$[C \oplus Z] = 1$	Branch if Lower or the Same (zero) (un-signed)

Unconditional Branch Instructions

BRA	(None)	BRanch Always
BRN	(None)	BRanch Never
BSR	(None)	Branch to SubRoutine

Note: All conditional branch instructions have both short and long variations.

the zero or **Z** bit. These are **BEQ** (**B**ranch if **EQ**ual to zero) and **BNE** (**B**ranch if **N**ot **E**qual to zero). If the test is true the program branches or skips over part of the program. The branch can be forward or backward. If the test was false the program continues in sequence. Therefore, when the subtraction instruction previously mentioned is followed by one of these conditional branch instructions, the state of the **Z** bit will determine the path to be taken by the program. This decision-making action is the primary function of a computer and is frequently

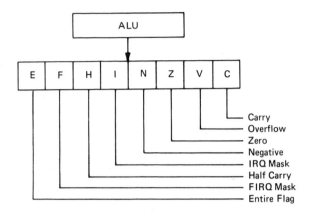

Figure 5.1 Condition Code Register

depicted in flow-charted programs by a diamond shaped box with an arrow out of the bottom to show the in-line sequence, or out of one side to show a branch. This is illustrated in Figure 5.2.

This figure shows a simple routine to clear 5 bytes starting at $1000. The **B** register is preset to 5 and decremented until it becomes zero. The **BNE** instruction is used to make the program loop back until the result of the decrement **B** is zero and the **Z** bit is SET by the ALU. It then goes in line sequence to the EXIT.

Each of the four least significant bits of the CCR (N, Z, V and C) has two branch instructions associated with it as shown in Table 5.1. Note that two of the opcodes have two names **(BCC, BHI and BCS, BLO)**.

Other conditional branch instructions use combinations of these status bits for more complex decisions and are also shown in Table 5.1. The way in which the bits are tested is ex-

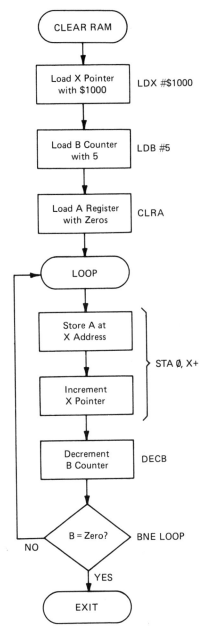

Figure 5.2 Using Branches

95

plained with *Boolean Algebra* formulas. This is another subject that will not be covered in detail here. The data sheets and other 6809 literature should be referenced. Note however, in the expression $(Z + C = 1)$ for the **BLS** instruction, the plus sign means **OR** in Boolean Algebra and means that a branch is taken if either the zero bit **or** the carry bit is a 1. The bits of the Condition Code Register are frequently also called *flags*). If neither flag is a 1, the microprocessor continues to the next instruction in sequence. The formulas for some of the conditional branch instructions shown in Table 5.1 use an *exclusive OR* symbol ($\oplus$). Some instructions are for dealing with *signed numbers* as used in two's complement arithmetic. (Bit 7 is a **1** for a negative number). All these factors are explained in detail in the 6909 programming manuals and data sheet.

The programmer uses these decision-making instructions to create the logic of the program. By adding, subtracting or comparing values in the registers or by simply loading the registers from memory or an I/O port, the status bits of the CCR are altered. The conditional branch instructions are then selected to cause the program to flow as desired. For example, in the case of the Industrial Control system we are describing, the microprocessor can be used with the conditional branch instructions described above to compare the measured heater temperature, with the desired set-point temperature. If they don't compare, the valves are adjusted appropriately to correct the temperature. If the temperatures are the same, (i.e., zero difference), the microcomputer can go on to other tasks such as monitoring the emissions and deciding whether the fuel/oxygen ratio must be adjusted. It is in the selection of these types of instructions that mistakes are occasionally made, and since debugging is the main purpose of this book we will suggest ways to find these problems and fix them.

REGISTER
ORGANIZATION

Before beginning to write any Assembly Language program, it is necessary to know a number of things about the microprocessor that will be used. In this case it is the 6809. Perhaps the first step is to study the register structure. Figure 5.3 shows the programming model of the 6809 Registers. The two index registers (X and Y), make it easy to move data (from table to table), in a straight-forward way.

STACK OPERATION

The use of a *stack* is not new for microprocessors but the 6809 has two stacks and therefore has added capability. A stack has several important uses. The stack is an area of memory where temporary data is kept. The two stacks are called the *User Stack*

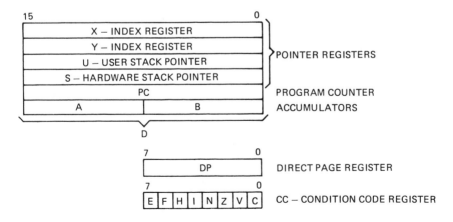

Figure 5.3 M6809 Programming Model

and the *Hardware Stack*. The processor uses the hardware stack during *subroutine* calls and interrupts. A subroutine call, such as **JSR, BSR,** or **LBSR** places the return address on the stack, and the **RTS** at the end of each subroutine uses it to return to the main program at the point following the original call. Interrupts also *stack* the registers on the hardware stack until they are restored by the **RTI** instruction at the end of the *interrupt service routine*. Stack Pointer Registers are used to keep track of the addresses, register contents, or other information in or *on the stack*. The *User stack pointer* (U) is controlled entirely by the programmer thus allowing *arguments* to be passed to and from subroutines with ease. The stacks can also be used to temporarily store data by means of the *push* and *pull* instructions. It is suggested that the users study the 6809 Data Sheet and/or Programming manuals for more details.

DEBUGGING

The techniques of debugging are best learned by doing. The first step is to study the Microcomputer Development System (MDS) manuals. The features provided in MDS units are similar, with most of them being provided primarily by the control or *monitor* program. In order to provide clear information we will describe the Motorola EXORciser with which we are most familiar. In this MDS, the control program is called EXbug, and it will be found that its many features serve to aid the designer in finding the cause of problems. Table 5.2 shows the EXbug commands and is helpful to quickly see the capability of the EXORciser.

The basic functions needed in any MDS are:

1. Single-step (;N)

2. Breakpoint (n;V)

3. Register Display/Change (;R), (.P), (.S), etc.)

4. Memory Display/Change (addr/)

The expression in brackets following each function is the EX-bug syntax for these commands.

It is possible to build a hardware circuit which will cause a microprocessor to execute one instruction at a time and to display the state of the address and data lines after each step. However, this is not very useful because it is not possible to also see the contents of the registers within the microprocessor. The EXbug program has this added capability of displaying these registers. The contents of the registers are kept in locations in RAM, known as Pseudo Registers. They are then updated and displayed when certain commands are used. These include Single-step, *Breakpoints*, the Register Display/Change command, and the ABORT function. For example, the Single-step command, when executed, puts the contents of the Pseudo Registers into the microprocessor's registers, executes the instruction pointed to by the Program Counter (PC) register, updates the Pseudo Registers, and then displays their contents. This command is probably the most useful of all to analyze each instruction but to look at every instruction in this way would take a prohibitive amount of time. If we were to single-step through the hundreds of thousands of instructions that would normally be executed in one second, it could take weeks. Therefore, other methods such as the breakpoint function are used initially to find the parts of the program that fail to run

TABLE 5.2

EXbug Commands

Command	Explanation
EXEC return	Debug in the Executive map default).
USER return	Debug in the User map.
PRNT return	Print memory in both hexadecimal and ASCII format.
LOAD return	Load an object tape from the terminal to memory.
VERF return	Verify an object tape from the terminal against memory.
SRCH return	Search an object tape on the terminal.
PNCH return	Punch an object tape on the terminal from memory.
MDOS return	Set the EXEC mode, then jump to E800.
.A nn [byte] return	Display and change the A accumulator.
.B nn [byte] return	Display and change the B accumulator.
.C nn [byte] return	Display and change the condition code register.
.D nn [byte] return	Display and change the DPR register.
;E nn [byte] return	Display and change the second level SWI enable.
;G	Go (jump) to the target program at its restart address.
addr;G	Go (jump) to the target program at the specified address.

TABLE 5.2 *(continued)*

Command	Explanation
$H nnnn [addr] return	Enable and change the halt on address or scope sync.
;H	Disable the halt on address and scope sync.
byte;I	Initialize memory with a specified byte.
;K nnnn [value] return	Display and change the terminal null pad value.
addr;L	Calculate long relative offset from currently open location to the specified location.
$M or ;M	Display and change the memory search beginning and ending addresses and search mask.
;N	Trace the next instruction.
value;N	Trace the next specified number of instructions.
addr; O	Calculate short relative offset from currently open location.
.P nnnn [addr] return	Display and change the program counter.
;P	Proceed with program execution.
value;P	Proceed with program execution from breakpoint; value specifies the number of times the breakpoint location is to be passed before returning control to EXbug and providing a register printout.

(continued)

TABLE 5.2 *(continued)*

Command	Explanation
;Q nnnn [value] return	Display and change the default debug offset.
$R or ;R ·	Display the target program registers.
.S nnnn [addr] return	Display and change the stack pointer.
$T nnnn [addr] return	Enable and change the trace to ending address.
;T	Disable the trace ending address.
.U nnnn [addr] return	Display and change the U register.
;U	Remove all breakpoints.
addr;U	Remove a specified breakpoint.
$V or ;V	Display the breakpoint addresses.
addr;V	Set a breakpoint at the specified address.
byte;W	Search memory for the specified byte (word). See the M command.
.X nnnn [addr] return	Display and change the X index register.
.Y nnnn [addr] return	Display and change the Y index register.
;Z nn [byte] return	Copy terminal output to printer option.
;:	Display the memory parity error interrupt.
;;	Enable the memory parity error interrupt.
Control-X	Abort the current command or entry.

TABLE 5.2 *(continued)*

Command	Explanation
Control-W	Wait until some other character is entered.
addr/nn cmnd	The memory change function is invoked by entering addr/. Cmnd is one of the following memory change function commands. These commands are accepted as long as EXbug remains in the memory change function.
[byte] LF	Change memory if byte entered, and display the next sequential location.
[byte] space	Change memory if byte entered, and display the previous sequential location.
[byte]/	Change memory if byte entered, and redisplay the current location.
[byte] return	Change memory if byte entered, and exit the memory change function.

a. Hexadecimal numbers may be preceded by a minus sign to obtain the two's complement of the value entered.

b. Values shown in brackets ([]) in above explanations indicate optional user inputs.

c. When addr is a single number (e.g., 142), the debug offset is added to the number to determine the value used by the command. If two comma-separated values are entered, the sum of the values is used by the command.

properly. The Breakpoint function enables the user to run portions of the program in real time (full speed) and to halt it at any instruction desired. It is only necessary to enter the instruction's address (using the nnnn;V command), and then start execution at an address prior to the breakpoint. Up to eight addresses can be entered into the breakpoint table at one time. The program runs until it encounters one of the breakpoints. It then displays all of the registers and returns to the EXbug program (prints the prompt and waits for a new command). The breakpoint table can be displayed by using the $V command.

Figure 5.4 shows a sample program and the procedure for using breakpoints. The sample program is a simple routine to get a character from an ACIA, as entered on a keyboard, and store it in a buffer. The keyboard could, for example, be the Burr-Brown Microterminal connected to one of the serial ports of the single board computer module. The program is loaded into memory, either by typing it in with the Memory Display/Change command, or loading it from the Floppy Disk system. The listing is shown in Figure 5.4a and the EXORciser terminal display is shown in 5.4b. In this subroutine, the first three instructions are intended to scan the ACIA's status register, and check the Receive Data Register Full (RDRF) flag repeatedly until a character is received. When the character is entered, the *RDRF* bit of the status word is SET and, when this word is shifted right by the **ASRA** instruction, it SETs the carry bit. The **BCC** (Branch if Carry is Clear) instruction will keep branching back to get the status, again and again, until a character is entered. This is called *looping*. It is virtually impossible to catch the status bit change as it is happening, so the breakpoint address is placed just after this loop. After entering the start address in the PC register (using .P), a ;P is entered

```
3000 B6   EC14   INCH   LDA $EC14   GET ACIA STATUS
3003 47                 ASRA        SHIFT BITS RIGHT
3004 24   FA            BCC INCH    LOOP TIL CARRY SET
3006 B6   EC15          LDA $EC15   GET CHARACTER
3009 84   7F            ANDA #$7F   MAKE BIT 7 ZERO
300B BE   1000          LDX SAVEX   GET BUFFER POINTER
300E A7   80            STA 0,X+    STORE CHAR - INDEX X
3010 BF   1000          STX SAVEX   SAVE POINTER
3013 39                 RTS         RETURN TO CALLER
```

a. Sample subroutine program

```
EXBUG09 2.1
E* 3006;V
E* $V 3006 0000 0000 0000 0000 0000 0000 0000
E* .P XXXX 3000
E* ;P     (waits here until character typed)
P-3006 X-XXXX Y-XXXX U-XXXX A-C1 B-XX C-E4 DP-00 S-FF8A
E* ;N
P-3009 X-XXXX Y-XXXX U-XXXX A-C1 B-XX C-E4 DP-00 S-FF8A
E* 3013;V
E* ;P
P-3013 X-1001 Y-XXXX U-XXXX C-41 B-XX C-E4 DP-00 S-FF8A
E*     (waits for next command)
```

    X's indicate random value. Operator entries are underlined.

    b. EXORciser terminal display

Figure 5.4 Program and Terminal Printout when using Breakpoints

to Proceed. This starts the program to execute but it will run around in a loop of the first three instructions until a key is pressed on the Microterminal keyboard (this is not the same one as used for the EXORciser). When a character is entered, the breakpoint will occur, which means that the EXbug program will display the registers, display the prompt, and wait for new commands. The user's program will now be stopped at the **LDA $EC15** instruction. If ;N is now entered, and the redisplayed registers examined, the **A** register will contain (**$C1**), the character that caused the break. Since many keyboards generate *parity* bits the MSB may be SET. If so, running the next instruction would clear it. Instead let's speed things up by putting a breakpoint at $3013 (at the **RTS**), and use ;P again. This will instantly run the next four instructions to store the character in the buffer at the location that was in

SAVEX. It will have incremented SAVEX, as seen in Figure 5.4b. Placing the breakpoint at the **RTS** was a good choice since the **RTS** should not be executed. This is because the routine was entered directly for these tests and did not get called by a subroutine call (**JSR** or **BSR**) as it normally would have been. (The return vectors do not exist on the stack.)

Normally, the entire breakpoint procedure would be as follows:

1. The object program which has been assembled previously is loaded into the MDS memory from the floppy disk system.

2. The Memory Display/Change routine is used to observe that the program is loaded properly and matches the listing. (A few places near the start and end are examined.)

3. Starting the program to freely execute is unwise because odds are that it will not work very well and may erase or modify itself, or cause damaging signals to be sent to the external hardware.

4. Insert a breakpoint at the end of the initialization routine or, if it is segmented, at the end of one segment. The program is then entered (using ;G or ;P). When the breakpoint is reached, EXbug resumes operation and the registers are all displayed. But more importantly, the function that was initialized should be examined with the Memory Display/Change routine to see if the desired results have been accomplished. For example, perhaps a section of RAM

must be cleared (made zero). It would be wise to look at the starting and ending addresses of the area involved to see if all the desired bytes were properly zeroed. It is likely that the first one or last one was missed. This is easily done if the wrong conditional branch instruction is used.

5. If everything works properly, a new breakpoint can be inserted further into the program and the next section checked. If, on the other hand, results were not as expected the breakpoint can be moved closer to the beginning until the breakpoint is properly reached. Then the Run-One-Instruction function is used to find the improper instruction or omission in the section that did not work. Another feature of the breakpoint command is the ability to defer the register display until the program has looped through a breakpoint a specified number of times. For example, in the subroutine of Figure 5.4, if a breakpoint is placed at $3010 ($3010;V), and is followed by: 5;P, it will only display the registers after it has stored the fifth character. This assumes that this subroutine was called by the main program and returns to be called again for each character. The advantage of this feature can best be appreciated where a program must loop through a routine a large number of times. Since a common fault is to go around the loop one too many or one too few times, it is easy to test the last time around with this feature. When testing the decision instructions, the simplest way is to use the breakpoint function. In an area where trouble is being experienced, a breakpoint can be placed in each path to determine which path is being taken.

The Register Display/Change command is useful to set up registers for testing one or more instructions without running through the entire program to get there. This is sometimes desirable when repeatedly testing a group of instructions to find the proper corrections. A program should always initialize the registers properly when entered at the proper starting point, so this use of the command is not normally necessary.

The Memory Display/Change command is useful to manually enter small program segments for test or to set or read memory locations used to hold data. It also is very useful to program and read peripheral registers such as those in the ACIA, PIA, or PTM devices. The command has the feature that it reads and verifies each location when used. This is not apparent when used with normal memory but when addressing a PIA control register or ACIA registers, for example, the number read may not match the value entered (this is explained in the sections where these devices are described). In this case, the Display/Change function will print a "?", sound the terminal Bell, and display what was read. If, for example, a $25 is written to a PIA control/status register where the MSB status bit is SET, the terminal will beep, print a "?", and display $A5. This will occur because, as stated previously, the status bits can only be cleared by reading the data register.

SOFTWARE PATCHES

At this point we should point out that the use of RAM in the MDS to hold the entire program allows us to change bytes, insert breakpoints, or, as will be explained, to *patch* the program to correct its operation. As each bug is located it should be carefully marked on the listing. When a number of bugs have been found, or if an error is found that requires more than twenty or so bytes to be changed or added, the program should be re-edited and reassembled. If only a few byte changes are needed, the debugging can continue, perhaps until it is time to go home. At any time desired, the program can be saved on the floppy disk by means of the ROLLOUT command of the disk operating system, (or on tape, if an appropriate terminal is being used), and can be reloaded later for continued debugging. When an erroneous instruction is found and the instructions required to correct it fit in the same locations it is not a problem, but if they will not fit, a *patch* is required. If fewer bytes are needed, **NOP** instructions ($12) are used to fill the unneeded bytes. If more bytes are required than space will permit then a patch can be installed by placing an instruction in the main program to cause a jump to a vacant area of memory where the added instructions can be written along with the instructions that were displaced by the jump. An example of this is shown in Figure 5.5

Figure 5.5a shows a typical keyboard input program which uses a PIA (the keyboard provides parallel information). To illustrate forgotten instructions, let us assume that we want to add two instructions to ignore the control characters (those with ASCII codes below $20), when they are entered on the keyboard. In this example we chose to replace the **CMPA #$D** and part of the **BEQ** instruction with a jump (**JMP**) to a free area beyond the end of the program. The patch instructions are shown located at address $3000. See Figure 5.5b. Note that the instructions that were displaced are reentered except that the second one is changed to an **LBEQ** (instead of **BEQ**). This is necessary because the patch area is out of range for a sim-

```
1000 B6 E001    CG     LDA $E001 GET PIA STATUS
1003 2B FB             BMI CG    NO CHAR - LOOP
1005 B6 E000           LDA $E000 GET CHAR
1008 81 0D             CMPA #$D CR ?
100A 27 20             BEQ CRLF ADD LF
100C .. ..             ... ....
     .. ..             ... ....
                       RTS

102C 86 0A     CRLF    LDA #$A GET LF
102E BD F018           JSR OUTCH OUTPUT IT
1031 86 0D             LDA #$D GET CR
1033 BD F018           JSR OUTCH OUTPUT IT
1035 39                RTS
```

a. Original program

```
1005 B6 E000           LDA $E000 GET CHAR
1008 7E 3000           JMP PATCH
100B 20
100C .. ..             ... ....

3000 81   0D   PATCH   CMPA #$D CR ?
3002 1027 102C         LBEQ CRLF GO ADD LF
3006 81   1F           CMPA #$1F CONTROL CHAR ?
3008 102D 1000         LBLT CG   YES-IGNORE IT
300E 7E   100C         JMP $100C RETURN FM PTCH
```

b. Revisions to Original program and added patch

Figure 5.5 Parallel keyboard program showing PATCH methods

ple branch. The desired additional instructions are now added, and as before, the long branch is used. These instructions test each character and when the hex value is greater than $1F ($20, $21, etc.), the program continues in sequence. If it is less than $20, a branch is made back to the start of the routine, effectively ignoring the control character. This is done only when printing or displaying the characters, of course. The last instruction of the patch jumps back to continue the original routine. After testing, and when the program is reassembled, these instructions will be inserted as in-line code in the original routine and will use simple branch instructions.

PATCHING BRANCH INSTRUCTIONS

Because short branch instructions have only a one byte *offset* (the second byte of the two byte instruction), and it is a two's complement number, the branch is limited to a range of plus 127 ($7F) or minus 128 ($80) locations (counted from where the program counter would normally be if it did not branch). (i.e., from the following opcode location). Bit 7 is the sign bit and the other 7 bits are the magnitude of the offset. This is shown in Figure 5.6.

1000	A6	80	LOOP	LDA	0,X+
1002	81	0D		CMPA	#$D
1004	27	02		BEQ	CR
1006	20	F8		BRA	LOOP
			*		
1008	··	··	CR	···	

Figure 5.6 An example of branching offsets

This is not an example of efficient code since the **BEQ CR** and **BRA LOOP** could be replaced with **BNE LOOP** and will save two bytes. These offsets are calculated by the Assembler program when the original program is generated but there are two EXbug functions (of the Memory/Display command), that are very useful when patching a program. These are the offset calculations (;O and ;L). They will calculate the required offset value (second byte of a simple branch or third and fourth bytes of most long branch instructions). The **LBRA** and **LBSR** are exceptions and have only three bytes altogether. When the ;O is used, the routine may show an *out of range* message, in which case the ;L (long branch) is used instead. When the operation of the patched program is verified, the program can be reassembled with the instructions inserted in sequence and branch, instead of long branch instructions used to minimize the number of bytes. The debugging can then continue with the reassembled version.

TYPICAL SOFTWARE ERRORS

Common faults found when debugging an object program are:

1. Inverted logic (**BNE** where **BEQ** should be).

2. Branching to wrong point.

3. Forgotten instructions (memory or registers not cleared, or set to prescribed values).

4. Failure to use correct addressing mode.

5. Looping once too few, or once too often.

An example of using the wrong addressing mode is where direct addressing is used instead of immediate addressing. (It is easy to forget the # sign.) For example, if the program needed to load the **A** register with the hexidecimal number $EF, the instruction, in assembly language, would be **LDA #$EF**. However, if **LDA $EF** was entered instead, then when the program is executed, the **A** register will be loaded with the contents of location $EF. This could cause strange things to happen, depending on the contents of that location. The difficulty in finding these types of programming errors depends on how the value $EF was to be used.

DEBUGGING
PROGRAMS WHICH
USE INTERRUPTS

The debugging described so far has been for situations where hardware interrupts have not been used. The EXbug program itself does not use the maskable hardware interrupts. This leaves the IRQ and FIRQ interrupts for use by the user's system. The EXORciser has several features, however, to aid in the evaluation of interrupts. If the user's system uses interrupts, it is necessary to disable them, or at least make certain they are *masked*, while the interrupt service routine is initially tested. Once it appears to be correct, the interrupt can usually be allowed to happen, under controlled conditions. Interrupt testing is more difficult because there usually is a need to process information quickly enough to keep up with something that is happening in the external hardware. When the program is waiting for another EXbug command, it is not able to process user program interrupts.

It should be noted that when program control returns to EXbug, after running a user instruction, it puts away the updated user program status (including the mask bits of the CCR), into memory locations known as the Pseudo Registers. The EXbug stack is also substituted while running EXbug instructions. When a Single-Step or Breakpoint command is started, the user's registers are restored to the MPU, and if the user's program had previously unmasked the interrupts, the next user instruction will be handled with the bits as set in the user's CCR.

EXORciser II provides for the use of NMI and SWI features by the user program without restricting their use by EXbug. This is known as the Second Level interrupt feature. It is described in the EXORciser manual. When one of these interrupts occur, EXbug functions are given first priority, but if it is found that the interrupt came from the user's system it will be serviced. This assumes that the service routine vector has been properly placed in the second level table. In many cases this will permit analysis of the user's program without difficulty but unfortunately a delay in responding (about 200 ms) will cause problems in some systems. This delay is included to accommodate some slower terminals. The delay can be avoided by substituting the user's vectors at the real vector locations ($FFF6 to $FFFF) in place of EXbug's vectors. This, of course, will disable the EXbug functions that use those vectors. The thing to do in this case, is to carefully debug the service routines (before the vectors are changed), with the mask SET or by disconnecting the hardware line that causes the interrupt. After assuring that the routines appear to do the right thing, the lines can be reconnected and the system allowed to execute the interrupt. It may be possible to insert **JMP** instructions to return to EXbug after a small part of the service routine is executed. Each case must be analyzed, to determine whether any harm is done to the external hardware by partial operation of some of the system.

CHAPTER 6
INITIAL
HARDWARE/SOFTWARE
TESTING AND FINAL
SYSTEM EMULATION

We have discussed the techniques of assembling the hardware in the EXORciser and verifying the electrical operation of the system components. We also have described software development and the use of the EXORciser debugging techniques. At this point we will discuss the development of software routines with which to exercise the hardware automatically, instead of manually.

Initially, a newcomer to microcomputers will probably want to test out various concepts before building anything. The ability to do this is one of the advantages of using a Microcomputer Development System such as the EXORciser.

We will assume that the things learned by exercising the hardware manually, has helped us to start writing the system operating program. To guide us in writing the program, and to keep track of our overall goals, a system level software flow chart should be developed. Since this book is aimed at explaining debugging techniques, we have elected to defer these diagrams and their explanation to Appendix A. Using these charts, modular pieces of the program can be assembled and tested one at a time as the system is developed. This will simplify the systems testing which must ultimately be done.

**VALVE HARDWARE/
SOFTWARE TESTING**

The program listing shown in Figure 6.1 is our first example. As seen in the System Flow Chart in Appendix A, initialization of the system hardware is done first. This example does not include initialization for the whole system. At first we are concerned about how to adjust the fuel and oxygen valves, which are controlled by the PIA, so the PIA is initialized (or programmed), to make the selected lines behave as required. The required control words were determined and verified manually in the discussions in Chapter 4. We now want to develop the program to provide the initialization for the valve subsystem when the system is turned on. As seen in the program listing of Figure 6.1, the PIA register addresses are given mnemonic names or *labels*. (PIADDB for Data/Direction and PIACSB for Control/Status. Both end in **B** because they designate the **B** side of the PIA). Reference to the 6821 Data Sheet shows that there are actually six registers in the PIA but as seen from the Data Sheet and the following, only four addresses are needed. Bit 2 of the **B** side Control/Status Register (at $EC13 in MM17) selects whether the Direction or the Data register will be accessed at address $EC12. Bits 6 and 7 of the register at $EC13 are really status bits while bits 0 through 5 are control bits which is why it is called a Control/Status register. These two most significant bits can not be changed by writing to the register. They are SET when one of the interrupt functions occurs, and cleared (RESET) by reading the data registers as noted in the data sheet. The **A** side of the PIA is identical and its three registers respond to their addresses in the same way.

The PIA has a hardware RESET pin which is connected to the reset line of the module. This pin is pulled low by an MC1455 timer whenever the power is applied to the module or the RESET switch is depressed. This, in turn, clears all PIA registers and, since bit 2 of the Control/Status register is also cleared, selects the Direction register. The Direction register is also cleared so the PIA I/O lines are programmed as inputs. When the reset line is released, the MPU places the RESTART vector into the Program Counter (PC) register and starts program execution at that address.

This test program has two basic subroutines INIT and KEY. They are called by the routine with the START label.

```
Line Addr Code      Label     OP    Operand        Comments

1                              NAM VALVES
2                   * TEST PROGRAM TO INITIAL AND EXORCISE
3                   * THE VALVE SUBSYSTEM
4                   *
5         EC10      PIADDA    EQU   $EC10          Data/Direction register
6         EC11      PIACSA    EQU   $EC11          Control/Status register
7         EC12      PIADDB    EQU   $EC12          Data/Direction register
8         EC13      PIACSB    EQU   $EC13          Control/Status register
9                   *
10        F012      INCHNP    EQU   $F012          EXbugs Input Character
11                  *
12                  * Vector Initialization
13                  *
14        FFF6                ORG   $FFF6
15  FFF6 0002       FIRQ      RMB   2
16  FFF8 0002       IRQ       RMB   2
17  FFFA 0002       SWI       RMB   2
18  FFFC 0002       NMI       RMB   2
19  FFFE 3037       RESET     FDB   START
20                  *
21                  * PIA Initialization
22                  *
23        3000                ORG   $3000
24                  *
25  3000 860F       INIT      LDA   #$0F
26  3002 B7EC12               STA   PIADDB         Set B side Directions
27  3005 862D                 LDA   #%00101101
28  3007 B7EC13               STA   PIACSB         Select CA1, CA2 modes
29  300A 39                   RTS
30                  *
31                  * OXYGEN VALVE COMMANDS
32                  *
33  300B 86FD       OCCW      LDA   #%11111101
34  300D B4EC12               ANDA  PIADDB         Turn OFF bit 1
35  3010 200C                 BRA   R1
36                  *
37  3012 8603       OCW       LDA   #%00000011
38  3014 BAEC12               ORA   PIADDB         Run Oxygen Valve CW
39  3017 2005                 BRA   R1
40                  *
41  3019 86FE       OSTOP     LDA   #%11111110
42  301B B4EC12               ANDA  PIADDB         Turn off Valve Motor
43  301E B7EC12     R1        STA   PIADDB         Send to valve
44  3021 39                   RTS
45                  *
46                  * FUEL VALVE COMMANDS
47                  *
48  3022 8607       FCCW      LDA   #%00000111
49  3024 B4EC12               ANDA  PIADDB         Switch to CCR
50  3027 20F5                 BRA   R1
51                  *
52  3029 860C       FCW       LDA   #%00001100
53  302B BAEC12               ORA   PIADDB         Run Fuel Valve CW
```

Figure 6.1 Valve Subsystem Test Program

```
54   302E  20EE              BRA    R1
55               *
56   3030  86FB      FSTOP   LDA    #%11111011
57   3032  B4EC12            ANDA   PIADDB          Stop Fuel valve motor
58   3035  20E7              BRA    R1
59               *
60   3037  10FE3FFF  START   LDS    $3FFF           Set up User Stack
61   303B  8DC3              BSR    INIT            Initialize PIA
62   303D  8D03              BSR    KEY             Go scan for Input
63   303F  7EF564            JMP    $F564           Return to EXbug
64               *
65               * Keyboard Routine
66               *
67   3042  BDF012    KEY     JSR    INCHNP          Input Character
68   3045  8141              CMPA   #'A             Is it an A ?
69   3047  271B              BEQ    A1              Yes - Run Oxygen valve CCW
70   3049  8142              CMPA   #'B             "B" ?
71   304B  271B              BEQ    B1              Yes - Run Oxygen valve CW
72   304D  8143              CMPA   #'C             "C" ?
73   304F  271B              BEQ    C1              Yes - Run Fuel valve CCW
74   3051  8144              CMPA   #'D             "D" ?
75   3053  271B              BEQ    D1              Yes - Run Fuel Valve CW
76   3055  8146              CMPA   #'F             "F" ?
77   3057  271C              BEQ    F1              Yes - Stop Fuel valve motor
78   3059  8147              CMPA   #'G             "G" ?
79   305B  271C              BEQ    G1              Stop Oxygen valve motor
80   305D  8145              CMPA   #'E             "E" ?
81   305F  2713              BEQ    E1              Yes Exit to EXbug
82   3061  26DF              BNE    KEY             None of the above
83   3063  39                RTS
84               *
85   3064  8DA5      A1      BSR    OCCW            Run Oxygen valve CCW
86   3066  20DA              BRA    KEY
87               *
88   3068  8DA8      B1      BSR    OCW             Run Oxygen valve CW
89   306A  20D6              BRA    KEY
90   306C  8DB4      C1      BSR    FCCW            Run Fuel valve CCW
91   306E  20D2              BRA    KEY
92               *
93   3070  8DB7      D1      BSR    FCW             Run Fuel Valve CW
94   3072  20CE              BRA    KEY
95   3074  39        E1      RTS                    RTN TO EXbug
96               *
97   3075  8DB9      F1      BSR    FSTOP           Stop Fuel valve motor
98   3077  20C9              BRA    KEY
99               *
00   3079  8D9E      G1      BSR    OSTOP           Stop Oxygen valve motor
01   307B  20C5              BRA    KEY
02               *
03                           END
***  TOTAL ERRORS      0--   0
***  TOTAL WARNINGS    0--   0
```

Figure 6.1 *(continued)*

This is technically the *Main* program. Note that the RESET vector gets set to the correct value by the FDB directive on line 19.

The STACK should be set to a suitable place in memory as a first step. This is necessary so that return addresses for subroutines will always be properly stored. This is followed by the branch to the initialization routine. The instruction on line 25 of the listing, loads the MPU's **A** register with $0F (00001111) which is then written to the PIA **B** side Direction register. That programs the 4 LSB I/O lines as outputs. The following instructions load **A** with $2D and stores it in the Control/Status register to select the data register (bit 2 is SET). Figure 6.2 shows that the other bits of the control word program the **B** side of the PIA so the CB2 line will be LOW, and the CB1 line will signal an interrupt if taken LOW. This line is pulled HIGH by a pullup resistor on the module and, since it is not connected to any external signal in our application, any false setting of the status bit (bit 6 of the Control/Status Register) is unlikely.

Although not the next step in the System Software Flow Chart (see Appendix A), it would be advisable to set up the routines for controlling the valves and complete their checkout before working with the **A** side of the PIA or other elements of the system. The valve control routines developed will be used as part of the main operating program.

The instructions for controlling the valves (see Figure 6.3) are selected by the following rules:

1. To turn OFF a control line (reset it to logic 0), the contents of the data register are ANDed with a zero bit in the appropriate position.

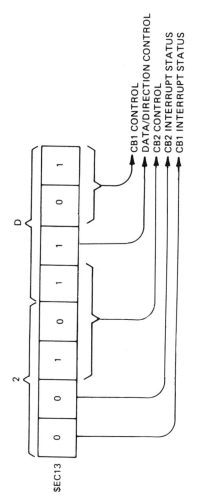

Figure 6.2 PIA Control/Status Register

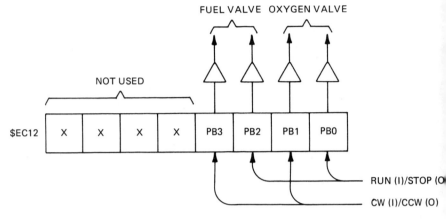

Figure 6.3 PIA B-Side Data Register Bit Assignment

2. To turn ON a control line (SET it to logic **1**), a 1 bit in the appropriate position is ORed with the existing contents of the data register.

The reason for using this **AND** and **OR** software technique is that we need to be able to independently control each control line to each valve. To do this the processor must read the current bit pattern, modify it, and write the modified bit pattern back to the PIA. For example:

ANDing **(ANDA PIADDB)**

XXXX1111 = contents of Data register at $EC12.

XXXX1101 = contents of MPU's **A** register.

———————

XXXX1101 = new *command word* which, when output, will switch the Oxygen valve from clockwise to counterclockwise.

In the meantime, the fuel valve is running clockwise. The Xs indicate *don't care* bits (can be **1s** or **0s**), since these lines are not used.

ORing **(ORAA PIADDB)**

XXXX1101 = contents of Data register

XXXX0010 = contents of MPU's **A** register

_____

XXXX1111 = new *command word* to start the Oxygen valve
clockwise, without affecting the Fuel valve.

The contents of the PIA data register is an indication of the status of the control lines. Note that the % symbol is used in writing these control words because it is much easier for the programmer to see which bits are set if he uses the binary form. The assembler will generate the hex form in the object code. Also note that the RUN/STOP signal is left ON (to RUN) whenever the direction line is changed. This simplifies programming but may not be compatible with the valve operation. It will be necessary for the designer to verify that this will not harm the valves and will work without unusual pertabations in the valve operation. It may be necessary to insert some delay between commands to allow the valve to stop before starting it again in the opposite direction.

It will help the designer to plan further if a temporary routine is written to partially automate the testing of the valve control subroutines. Such a keyboard routine is shown in Figure 6.1. To simplify this test program, a single letter is used to select the valve and direction. It's hard to assign the letters mnemonically, so a lookup table should be kept at hand. Note that after each letter is typed, the routine returns for the next command. Also, there is no protection to prevent the valves from running all the way open or closed. If this is apt to damage the valves, the testing will have to be very carefully done, or limited until the system is operational. In order to *close the loop* (i.e., provide feedback), the next step in the design process is to generate the preliminary programming for the flow monitor part of the system. As shown in Chapter 4 and in Figure 4.9, this part of the system is more complex. Figure 4.10 is a program to initialize and read the PTM. It will be seen that this program uses the information learned in Chapter 4. Also, it should be noted that the Main program will ultimately call all of the initialization routines before actually starting the system.

**EMULATION OF THE
FINAL SYSTEM**

When doing application software development in the MDS, the programs are loaded into RAM for testing and, in effect, are used to emulate the final EPROMs or ROMs. The use of RAM also allows breakpoints and patches to be inserted. The program is subject to many changes when first assembled, and it would be foolish to go to the trouble and cost of putting the program into EPROM or ROM until it is completely debugged. When beginning the development of an applications program, usually, little is known about its ultimate size and therefore it is not known where the final program EPROMs will reside in the system memory map. After all subsystems have been implemented and performance verified, it is possible to begin planning how to package the program. It undoubtedly should be transferred to EPROM for final systems testing and preliminary operation. After suitable verification and if many identical systems are planned, masked ROMs can be used for the production versions.

Depending on the size of the program, it may be possible to place it in one 2K, 4K, or 8K EPROM. If certain parts of the final system are modular and there is any possibility of replacing one subsystem with another type, it may be appropriate to segment the firmware into several 2K, or 4K EPROMs. In any event, once the program size is known, the possible location(s) in MM17 can be determined. If the program is less than 4K in size, it can be placed either in two 2K parts or in one 4K part in the sockets of MM17. One of these ROM (or EPROM) sockets is connected to provide memory at the top of the MM17 memory map ($FFFF). It is necessary to include the RESTART vector in this EPROM so it will be at $FFFE. If the size of the program does not exceed 4K, it is possible to assemble the program in one contiguous block in the $F000 to $FFFF range. If the program size exceeds 4K, it will have to be segmented and part of it located in one of the sockets which are addressed below $E000. The separation is necessary if the standard MM17 address decoder is to be used, since the standard configuration places the RAM at $E000 to $E7FF and the I/O and timer at $EC00 to $EC1F. This segmentation of the program in order to work with the standard decoder should not be a problem and can be accomplished by selecting suitable **ORG** statements when assembling the program.

It is possible, of course, to make up a special address decoder which locates the I/O at a lower address. This would require more testing before finalization because of the additional changes and subsequent increase in the probability of mistakes. Also, if many systems are to be built, the cost of reprogrammed decoders must be considered. Once the memory configuration is selected and reassembly of the program done with the appropriate **ORG** statements, EPROMs can be made. This can be done by using the EXORciser family PROM programmer or stand-alone units such as Data I/O, etc. It's also possible to have the EPROMs programmed by your local electronics distributor.

Once these EPROMs are made and installed, it should be possible to place the switch at the top of the Debug Module to the USER position and start the system simply by turning on the power or pushing RESTART. This will fetch the User's Restart Vector from address $FFFE and $FFFF, load it into the Program Counter Register and then start running the program. If the Restart Vector has been properly programmed into the EPROM, the system should start up and operate just as it did with the program in RAM. It is likely however, that some overseeing may prevent this, so continued debugging will need to be done. To do this and with the system still in the EXORciser, the Debug Module's switch is placed in the EXbug position. After typing USER, the Memory Display/Change command is used to see if the EPROMs can be read at the right address and that the Restart Vector is correct. The I/O devices should also be accessed to be sure nothing has happened to them in the course of reconfiguring. If the programs appear to be correct and all devices can be accessed properly, the program should run when entered. If it doesn't run properly, it is possible to step through the program as before using ;N. However, it is not possible to use breakpoints because they require RAM. The Halt-On-Address feature is used instead. It provides the ability to run portions of the program as with breakpoints, except that the program will stop at the end of the instruction addressed instead of at its start.

USER SYSTEM EVALUATION

An alternate approach to *emulation* of the final system in the EXORciser is to use the User System Evaluator (USE) which was described in Chapter 4 and shown in Figure 4.6. This accessory is installed in the EXORciser and connects to the user's system by means of a cable which plugs into the MM17's 6809 socket in place of the MPU. The User System in this case is assembled in its own chassis. USE will allow debugging or operation of the User System in a manner that is almost identical to that previously described. The User System is still accessed in the USER map and all EXbug routines work as before.

After reconfiguring the system in this way, an additional feature is provided which makes debugging of ROMs or EPROMs easier. This feature allows the use of RAM in the EXORciser chassis at the same address as the Read-Only Memories in MM17. The USE System gives priority to the RAM so the EPROMs need not be removed or even disabled.

Thus, if the program will not run properly, or at all, after being placed in EPROMs, the same program can be loaded into the Development System RAM and Breakpoints or patches used to find the problems. It's not likely that major rework of the program is necessary at this stage in the development, but this technique will allow easier identification of the reasons why the reassemblies are not working.

One difficulty with this method is that the I/O addresses must not be overlayed by the MDS RAM. This might be difficult with large (32K) RAM modules. Some of the RAM modules for the EXORciser can be restrapped to enable portions of the total. This is possible with several versions of the Dynamic or Hidden Refresh memory modules, for example.

ABORTING A PROGRAM

At times, when a program is loaded into memory and not yet debugged, it may *bomb out*, or *run away* when an attempt is made to execute it. The program may modify itself or cause false operation of the hardware. This also frequently results in strange displays on the terminal, or no response from the keyboard. In any event, if the program does not reach a breakpoint or the hardware begins to operate peculiarly, the first thing to do is to quickly press the *ABORT* button. Most of the time this will result in a return to EXbug and a display of the user's registers. A study of the registers may disclose useful information as to why the program failed. The Program Counter value will show where the program was running, and the Stack Pointer should point to the user's stack area. If the Stack Pointer looks normal, that area of memory can be listed to see what return addresses are included. If the return addresses can be identified with the program instructions in a certain area, it may be possible to carefully reexamine them to find the cause of the difficulty. Sometimes, after the program has done something strange, the system will not respond when the ABORT button is pressed. In this case, the RESTART button must be used. (The ABORT button will not respond if the runaway program has wiped out the EXbug vectors.) In this case it is likely that other parts of the program will have been altered. Unless you feel you want to examine the existing code, it is advisable to reload your progam and make a fresh start. When in the process of debugging, ABORT should always be used first. Otherwise, valuable information (in the registers) may be lost. It should be noted, however, when running in MDOS, or certain other programs, ABORT can not be used because those programs have altered the NMI vector. RESTART will always restore EXbug's vectors so that the ABORT button as well as other debugging features will work. In a debugged program, an ABORT will stop the program and display the registers. Using ;P (proceed) will resume program execution from the point where it stopped.

SYSTEM ANALYZER

Still another debugging tool which can be used with the EXORciser, is the Systems Analyzer Module shown in Figure 6.4. This module is very useful for finding certain types of problems. One use is to step through some instructions manually when the 6809 will not run. It is sometimes possible to see the effects of shorted or grounded address or data lines. Another very interesting use is to take a *snapshot* of the program while it is running. This stores 128 cycles of program operation in RAM. It can then be printed out as a cycle-by-cycle trace. This

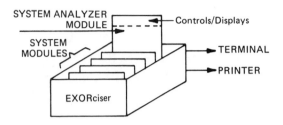

Figure 6.4 System Analyzer, In EXORciser

is very useful when it is not apparent why a program takes the path that it does. As seen in Figure 6.5, the analyzer has routines that will display 128 cycles of program operation on the CRT or print it on the printer. Each of the 128 cycles shows 32 bits of data which includes not only the states of the address and data lines, but also of the control lines such as NMI, R/W, HALT and IRQ. Up to four other signals can be monitored, including TTL level signals from the user's hardware. When something is happening that shouldn't, or something is not happening that should, it is often possible to track down the cause using the System Analyzer.

E ED00┆G

DDR DA VWNIUSER	ADDR DA VWNIUSER	ADDR DA VWNIUSER	ADDR DA VWNIUSER
FFE 00 10001111	FFFE 00 10001111	FFFE 00 10001111	FFFE 00 10001111
FFE 00 10001111	FFFE 00 10001111	FFFE 00 10001111	FFFE 00 10001111
FFE 00 10001111	FFFE 00 10001111	FFFE 00 10001111	FFFE 00 10001111
FFE 00 10001111	FFFE 00 10001111	FFFE 00 10001111	FFFE 00 10001111
FFE 00 10001111	FFFE 00 10001111	FFFE 00 10001111	FFFE 00 10001111
FFE 00 10001111	FFFE 00 10001111	FFFE 00 10001111	FFFE 00 10001111
FFE 00 10001111	FFFE 00 10001111	FFFE 00 10001111	FFFE 00 10001111
FFE 0C 10001111	FFFE 00 10001111	FFTC 00 10001111	FFFE 00 10001111
FFE 00 10001111	FFFE 00 10001111	FFFE 00 10001111	FFFE F0 10001111
FFE 00 10001111	FFFE 00 10001111	FFFE 00 10001111	FFFE F0 10001111
FFE 00 10001111	FFFE 00 10001111	FFFE 00 10001111	FFFE F0 10001111
FFE 00 10001111	FFFE 00 10001111	FFFE 00 10001111	FFFE F0 10001111
FFE 00 10001111	FFFE 00 10001111	FFFE 00 10001111	FFFE F0 10001111
FFE 00 10001111	FFFE 00 10001111	FFFE 00 10001111	FFFF 00 10001111
FFE 00 10001111	FFFE 00 10001111	FFFE 00 10001111	FFFF 00 10001111
FFE 00 10001111	FFFE 00 10001111	FFFE 00 10001111	F000 16 10001111

E ED03┆G

DDR DA VWNIUSER	ADDR DA VWNIUSER	ADDR DA VWNIUSER	ADDR DA VWNIUSER
000 16 10001111	F2E5 5E 10001111	F2BD AF 10001111	FFFF 00 10001111
001 02 10001111	F2B6 8E 10001111	FFFF 00 10001111	FFE6 00 11001111
002 A7 10001111	FFFF 00 10001111	FFFF 00 10001111	FFE7 00 11001111
FFF 00 10001111	FF00 83 11001111	F2BD AF 10001111	F2C4 ED 10001111
FFF 00 10001111	FF01 FF 11001111	F2BE 4E 10001111	F2C5 C4 10001111
2AA 10 10001111	F2B6 8E 10001111	F2BF 4F 10001111	F2C6 CE 10001111
2AB CE 10001111	F2B7 FB 10001111	FFFF 00 10001111	FF02 00 11001111
2AC FF 10001111	F2B8 61 11001111	FF10 FB 11001111	FF03 00 11001111
2AD E5 10001111	F2B9 AF 10001111	FF11 67 11001111	F2C6 CE 10001111
2AE CE 10001111	F2BA 4C 10001111	F2BF 4F 10001111	F2C7 FC 10001111
2AF FF 10001111	F2BB 30 10001111	F2C0 5F 10001111	F2C8 F4 10001111
2B0 02 10001111	FFFF 00 10001111	F2C0 5F 10001111	F2C9 CC 10001111
2B1 8E 10001111	FF0E FB 11001111	F2C1 FD 10001111	F2CA FF 10001111
2B2 83 10001111	FF0F 61 11001111	F2C1 FD 10001111	F2CB 3C 10001111
2B3 FF 10001111	F2BB 30 10001111	F2C2 FF 10001111	F2CC ED 10001111
2B4 AF 10001111	F2BC 06 10001111	F2C3 E6 10001111	F2CD 44 10001111

Figure 6.5 System Analyzer Cycle-by-Cycle Trace Printout

APPENDIX A
SYSTEM SOFTWARE
FLOWCHARTS

The first step in designing any system should be to develop a system level software flowchart like the one shown in Figure A.1 for this application example. This flowchart should contain the sequence of functions that the application software will follow during operation of the system. Specific details are not needed since detailed flowcharts of each function could, and should, be prepared.

As can be seen, the flowchart in Figure A.1 starts with initial power ON or system RESET and includes all of the func-

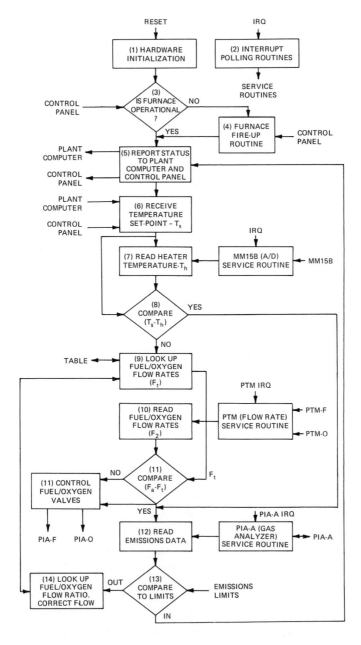

Figure A.1 Heater System Software Flow Diagram

tional steps and required decisions to maintain the proper operation of the plant heater. A detailed discussion of each functional block, keyed to the numbers in each block, along with its detailed flowchart follows:

1. **HARDWARE INITIALIZATION.** As discussed in Chapter 3, when the hardware has been reset by turning power ON or activating the RESET switch, a number of the hardware devices must be initialized by the software. That is, both halves of the PIA must be configured for proper operation, all three sections of the PTM must be configured to count the flow rate pulses as a function of time, the A/D converter must be setup for the required mode of operation and each ACIA must be programmed to match their required communications modes. When initializing the PIA, it is important that an output signal, which would cause the valves to operate, is not generated (see Figure A.2).

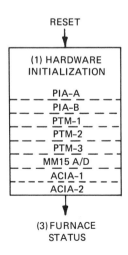

Figure A.2 Hardware Initialization

2. **INTERRUPT POLLING ROUTINES.** There are five potential sources that can generate an Interrupt ReQuest (IRQ) in this system as follows:

A. ACIA 1 — Bit 7 of the Status Register is the flag bit and is set by Transmit Data Register Empty, Receive Data Register Full or Data Carrier Detect indicating that there is no carrier from the modem (if used).

B. ACIA 2 — Same as ACIA 1.

C. PIA A Side — Bit 7 of the Control Register is the flag bit and is set by the Gas Analyzer when it has data available to be read.

D. PTM — Bit 7 of the Status Register is set by counter 1's Gate input indicating that Flow Rate data is available.

E. Micromodule 15B — Bit 7 of the Command/ Multiplex Channel Register is set by a completion of conversion indicating that analog data is available.

Since all five of these interrupt sources are tied to the common IRQ pin on the microprocessor, an Interrupt Polling Routine is required to determine the source of the interrupt. (See Figure A.3).

3. **IS FURNACE OPERATIONAL?** It is important, when turning the system on, that the controller be instrumented so it knows whether the pilot is lit and

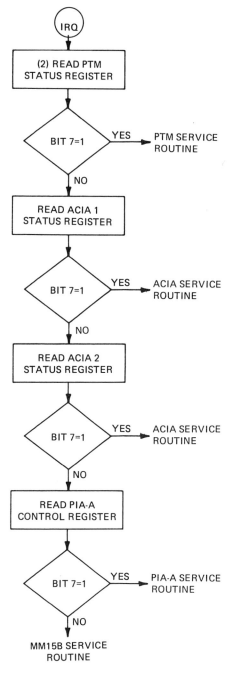

Figure A.3 Interrupt Polling Routine

the furnace is operational or not. If the furnace is not fired up and the controller were allowed to continue to feed in fuel, it could cause a very dangerous situation. Therefore, it is advisable to require that the plant engineer enter a command through the control panel Microterminal to allow further operation or to initiate the furnace fire-up routine (see Figure A.4).

4. **FURNACE FIRE-UP ROUTINE.** If the furnace has been turned off, then a routine to fire-up the

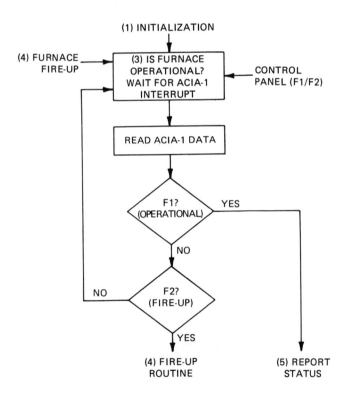

Figure A.4 Furnace Operational Status

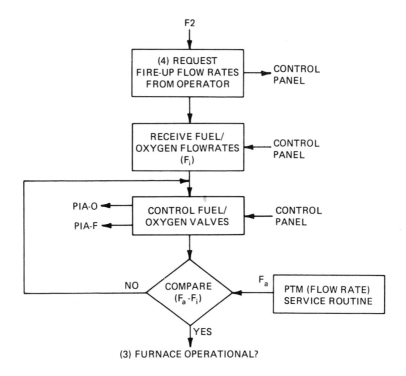

Figure A.5 Furnace Fire-Up Routine

furnace is required. Again, this is best handled by the plant engineer through the control panel. The Microterminal has eight function keys that can be used to initiate any desired operation. One of them can be used to turn on the fuel and oxygen valves, when the operator has determined that the igniting system is ready. Another function key can be used to resume normal control after the furnace has reached stable operation (see Figure A.5).

5. REPORT STATUS TO PLANT COMPUTER.

The status of the heater system needs to be reported

to the main plant computer. When the furnace has just been fired-up, the plant computer needs to be informed of that status so that it can provide the initial set-point temperature. Periodically, the plant computer may request from the controller, detailed status information on temperature, fuel and oxygen flow rates, and emissions. This information could also be displayed on the control panel (see Figure A.6).

6. **RECEIVE TEMPERATURE SET POINT — Ts.** Following a furnace startup, or whenever conditions dictate, the plant computer will transmit the desired operating set-point temperature to the controller. This information must be stored in memory for future reference. The plant engineer could also input the set-point temperature through the control panel (see Figure A.7).

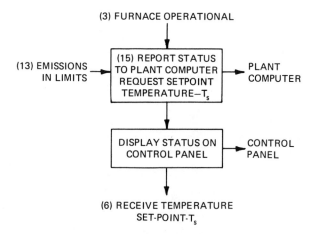

Figure A.6 System Status Reporting

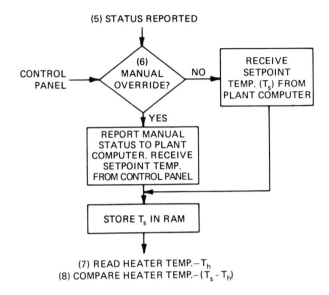

Figure A.7 Receive Temperature Setpoint-T_s

7. **READ HEATER TEMPERATURE — Th.** Whenever the control program loops around it will read the A/D converter data to determine the actual heater temperature. This information must be stored in memory for future reference (see Figure A.8).

8. **COMPARE (Ts-Th).** The actual heater temperature must be compared to the set-point temperature in order to determine if the fuel/oxygen flow rates need to be changed. It would not be practical to require that the two temperatures be identical or continuous adjustment of the flow rates would occur. A predetermined number of the least-significant bits could be masked from the comparison to provide a dead-band zone (see Figure A.9).

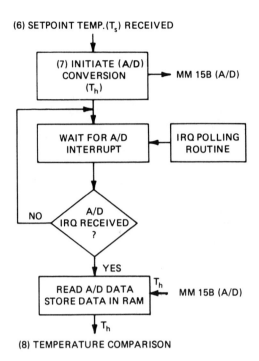

Figure A.8 Read and Store T_h

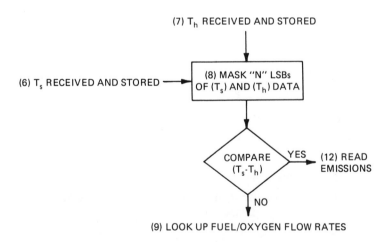

Figure A.9 Temperature Comparison

142

9. **LOOK UP FUEL/OXYGEN FLOW RATES.** A look-up table, based on either known or empirical data, that provides a fuel and oxygen flow rate vs. set-point temperature can be stored in memory. If the temperature comparison results in a difference, plus or minus, then this table can be read to determine the required flow rates. This data should be stored in RAM for future use (see Figure A.10).

10. **READ FUEL/OXYGEN FLOW RATES.** The two PTM sections that are being used to measure the fuel and oxygen flow rates have been read by the microprocessor and the resultant data stored in RAM. The latest flow rates will always be present in their RAM locations (see Figure A.11).

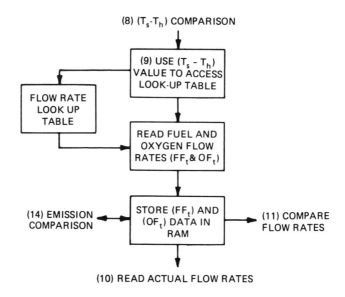

Figure A.10 Look Up Fuel/Oxygen Flow Rates

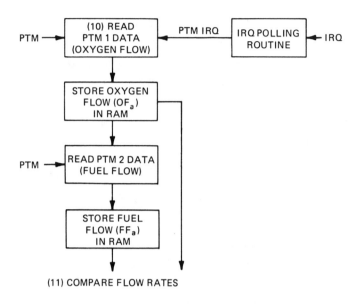

Figure A.11 Read Fuel/Oxygen Flow Rates

11. **COMPARE FLOW RATES (Fa-Ft).** The actual fuel and oxygen flow rates are compared with the table fuel and oxygen flow rates (Fa-Ft). Any differences will result in a need to adjust the fuel and/or oxygen valves. As in the temperature comparison, the least-significant bits can be masked (or ignored) to provide a dead-band zone where adjustment is not called for (see Figure A.12). It should also be noted that the table look-up techniques are normally used as an initial adjustment and the closed-loop nature of the system is used to refine the adjustments for optimum performance. Comparisons will result in either a positive, negative, or possibly zero difference. The difference is between the Actual Flow Rate and the Flow Rate from the table. A positive difference means the correspond-

ing fuel or oxygen flow rate must be reduced by commanding the appropriate valve to run counter-clockwise (close valve). A negative difference will require the valve to run clockwise (open valve). If a zero difference results no adjustment is made.

12. **READ EMISSIONS.** Once the flow rates are correctly established, the performance of the heater must be monitored and corrected if necessary. The PIA-A side is commanded to request emission data from the Gas Analyzer. This data is stored in RAM for further use (see Figure A.13).

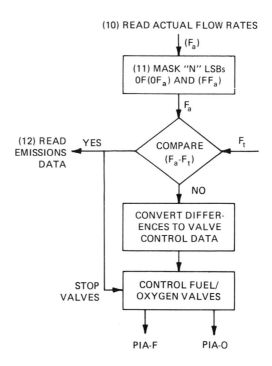

Figure A.12 Compare Flow Rates (F_a-F_t)

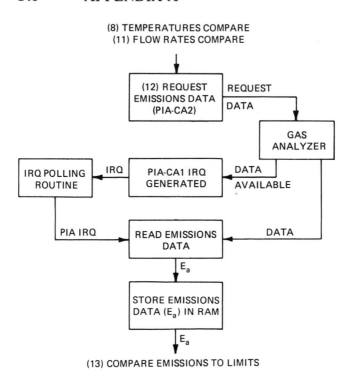

(8) TEMPERATURES COMPARE
(11) FLOW RATES COMPARE

(12) REQUEST EMISSIONS DATA (PIA-CA2)

REQUEST DATA

GAS ANALYZER

IRQ POLLING ROUTINE

IRQ

PIA-CA1 IRQ GENERATED

DATA AVAILABLE

PIA IRQ

READ EMISSIONS DATA

DATA

E_a

STORE EMISSIONS DATA (E_a) IN RAM

E_a

(13) COMPARE EMISSIONS TO LIMITS

Figure A.13 Read Emissions Data

13. **COMPARE TO LIMITS.** The results of the emissions data are compared to preestablished limits. If, for example, the Gas Analyzer indicates that excess oxygen is present then the proper fuel-to-oxygen ratio can be obtained from a look-up table, compared to the actual ratio and used to adjust the oxygen flow rate as required (see Figure A.14).

14. **LOOK UP FUEL/OXYGEN RATIO.** As previously mentioned, a table of fuel/oxygen ratios vs emissions performance is needed. This table can be

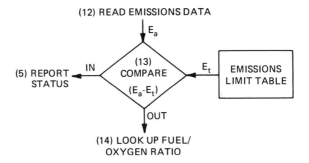

Figure A.14 Emission Comparison

established from known specification data or by empirical means. This table data may also require modifications as conditions change (see Figure A.15).

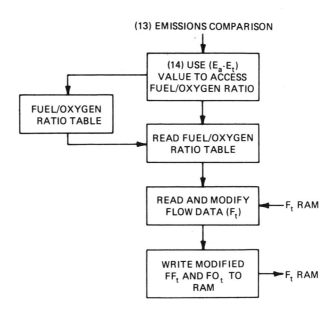

Figure A.15 Emission Correction

APPENDIX B
CLOSED-LOOP
SYSTEMS STABILITY
AND DYNAMICS

One of the fundamental problems associated with any adaptive or feed back control loop is system stability and dynamics. See Figure B.1. For example, this system operates just like the heater in your home. You set the desired temperature at the thermostat. If the set-point temperature is higher than the actual monitored temperature then the thermostat will turn on the heater. Ideally, the temperature would rise to precisely the set-point temperature and then the heater would be controlled

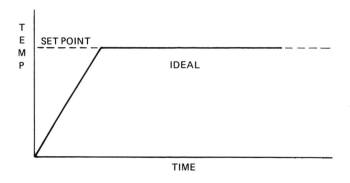

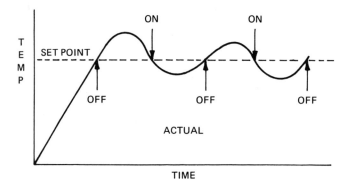

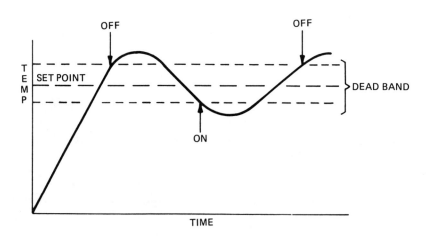

Figure B.1 System Dynamics

150

to maintain that fixed temperature. However, in reality this is not possible due to the system dynamics. If, for example, the thermostat were to turn off the heater when it detected that the set-point temperature was reached, the actual temperature would continue to rise beyond the set-point value. This would be due to such factors as the residual heat in the heater and in the physical space between the heater and the monitor, etc. Then, as the heater and its surrounding air space cooled off, the temperature would decrease below the set-point and the heater would be turned on again. This on-off cycling could occur quite rapidly, depending on the physical characteristics of the heater and its environment, and would be hard on the equipment. For this reason, a *dead-band* zone is designed into the system to allow acceptable variations around the set-point temperature.

In our example, the system dynamics are much more complex but the end result would be the same. The system would operate in an unstable fashion if these dynamic effects were not accounted for in the system design. Some of these dynamics are:

1. Rate of change of fuel/oxygen flow as a function of valve RUN commands.

2. Overrun of valve travel after a valve STOP command.

3. Flow rate errors due to time lag in making flow rate measurements.

4. Overshoot of actual temperature vs. set-point due to heater thermal lag characteristics.

5. Interactive effects between maintaining the temperature and minimizing the emissions.

If all of these dynamic characteristics were known there
are mathematical techniques that could be used to solve the
control equations. However, these techniques are beyond the
scope of this book. Even with theoretical control equations being used in the system, it would still require *tuning* during final
system testing.

While the control system is still in the development
configuration, that is, in the EXORciser or connected to the
EXORciser through the USE, it can be used to test and measure
some of these dynamic characteristics as follows:

1. The 10 second interrupt sequences from the flow-
   rate PTM operation can be used to start and then
   stop the valve controls to measure the flow-rate
   change as a function of valve control timing. This
   resulting information would include the effects of
   valve overrun, rate of change of fuel/oxygen (as a
   function of valve RUN commands), and the time lag
   of flow-rate measurement for comparison with the
   valve specifications.

2. A patched-in routine could be used to allow the operator to independently control the fuel and the oxygen valves. By controlling each valve for various
   flow rates, data can be accumulated and printed for
   fuel flow, oxygen flow, temperature, and emissions.

When sufficient data has been tabulated it can be used
to develop the preliminary look-up tables for the set-point con-

trol algorithm. This data can be further refined by then commanding various set-points and monitoring the operation to see if any unaccounted for dynamics tend to make the operation unstable. For example, the set-point temperature can be increased, and then decreased, in 10 degree increments over the operating range of the heater. Following each set-point change the operation of the valves can be monitored to see if either valve tends to *hunt* for its optimum position. If so, the system can be interrogated to determine what caused the hunting or instability. Once the look-up table parameters have been fine-tuned, they can be programmed into EPROM or be downloaded into the system from the main plant computer. Since these system dynamics may change over a period of time, this type of testing and tuning should be repeated periodically using the EXORciser and the USE module.

GLOSSARY

ABORT
A Microcomputer Development System function that allows the user to stop execution of his program and return control to the Monitor/control program. The EXORciser has a front panel ABORT switch.

ACIA
The Asynchronous Communications Interface Adapter — One of the 6800 family components, used for serial communications.

Address — Memory and Input/Output devices are connected so they have a unique location in the microcomputer's memory map.

Address Bus — The 16 lines used by the MPU to select the memory and I/O locations.

A/D — Analog-to-Digital — A circuit or module used to convert analog signals to digital values.

ALU — Arithmetic Logic Unit — Logic circuits in an MPU that perform the arithmetic and logic operations.

Analog — A type of electronic circuit which uses signals that are continuously variable.

Argument — Variable data used with a computer command.

ASCII — American Standard Code for Information Interchange — A seven-bit code that is used in serial communications to transmit character sets and control codes.

Assemble	The process in a microcomputer development system that translates Assembly Language mnemonics into microprocessor machine code.
Assembly Language	The mnemonic expressions used by a programmer, that are translated by the Assembler program to machine codes recognizable by the microcomputer.
Asynchronous	Not Synchronous — occurring randomly.
Base n	A number system with n values: Common values are: Binary ($n = 2$), Octal ($n = 8$), Decimal ($n = 10$), Hexidecimal ($n = 16$).
Basic	A high-level programming language.
Baud Rate	A term used to describe serial comunications transmission rates.
Binary	A number system with a base of 2, (**0** and **1**).

Bipolar — A type of Semiconductor construction used to make TTL ICs.

Bit — One binary digit (**1** or **0**).

Bit Manipulation — Using Assembly Language instructions that work on individual bits of control words or bytes.

Bomb-out — Computer jargon for a sudden change when a program starts doing things that it is not supposed to do. Usually caused by the use of improper instructions.

Boolean Algebra — A mathematical system used to analyze binary logic.

Branch — A computer instruction which causes the program to proceed out of normal sequence.

Breakpoint — A Microcomputer Development System Instruction that can be placed in a program to cause it to stop running the user programmed return to the monitor program.

Buffer — In Hardware: IC gates used to add greater drive or isolate an output or input signal. In Software: A section of memory set aside to temporarily store a line or many lines of data.

Bugs	Software or hardware errors that cause improper system operation.
Byte	A computer word made up of 8 bits.
Byte-wide	An 8 bit digital word or 8 lines of a bus taken together. A parallel view.
Card Cage	A mechanical housing and mother-board, used to house microcomputer modules.
CCR	Condition Code Register — An MPU register whose bits are set or reset as a function of the instruction just performed. May also provide some MPU control functions.
Chassis	Mechanical hardware that includes a Card Cage and a Power Supply.

Chip | An Integrated Circuit die cut from a silicon wafer.

Chip Set | A family of Integrated Circuit devices that were designed to work together.

Clock | An oscillator used to synchronize operations within a computer.

Closed Loop | A feedback system where information is returned to modify the control operation.

Compiler | A Microcomputer Development System program that converts High Level language instructions into assembly or machine language.

Control Bus | The lines used to control various functions in a microcomputer system. 12 lines for a 6809.

CPU | Central Processing Unit — The heart of a computer. Contains the ALU and other control and buffering circuits.

Crystal control   An element used in oscillator circuits to provide precise and stable frequencies.

CW/CCW   Clockwise/Counterclockwise-direction of rotation.

D/A   Digital-to-Analog — A circuit or module used to convert digital signals to an analog voltage (or current) equivalent.

Data Bus   The lines used to transfer data between devices in a computer. Eight lines are used in the 6809 Microcomputer systems.

Dead-band   An area between two limits where, normally, no action takes place.

Debugging   The process of finding, and correcting errors or bugs in a computer system's software and/or hardware.

Digital   A type of electronic circuit which uses signals with two discrete values (two-states).

Driver   In software, a modular subroutine
                          that controls the operation of I/O
                          devices. In hardware, an IC used
                          to provide additional power for
                          external devices.

Edge connector   An electrical connector built on
                          the edge of a PC board as an ex-
                          tension of the printed wiring. The
                          contacts are usually gold plated.

Editor   A Microcomputer Development
                          System program that provides for
                          writing and editing programs on a
                          terminal.

EIA   Electronic Industries Association
                          — An association that provides en-
                          gineering standards.

Emulate   To use a Microprocessor Develop-
                          ment System to take the place of
                          an MPU, so that debugging can
                          be done in the target system.

EPROM   Electrically Programmable Read
                          Only Memory. Erasable by Ultra
                          Violet Light.

Executive Map   One of two full 65536 byte memory maps provided in the EXORciser.

Family   A coordinated group of Integrated Circuit devices or modules which make up a Microcomputer.

FIRQ   One of the signal pins on a 6809 microprocessor. Used to input "Fast Interrupt Requests" from the external hardware.

Flag   A status bit in a RAM or register that indicates that an event has happened or a condition exits.

Floppy Disk Controller   An interface circuit, between the microcomputer and a floppy disk drive, that controls the read/write operation.

Flow Chart   A pictorial diagram of a process or program showing the sequence of steps and the decision points.

Fortran   A high level language favored by

some because of its scientific cal-
culation capabilities.

Handshake
A control technique for asynchronous transfer of data, normally
uses a data request signal and a
data available signal.

Hex
A commonly used abbreviation
for the Hexidecimal number system with a base of 16.

HIGH
One of two possible states of a
digital signal. Usually approxi-
mately equal to the supply voltage.

Hunt
A phenomenon in electrical or me-
hanical devices which tend to overshoot when seeking a new position.
They oscillate back and forth.
Caused by insufficient damping of
the resonate circuit.

IC
Integrated Circuit—A Semiconductor device.

Initialization
A computer software routine that
configures the computer hardware

so that it performs the desired function.

Interrupt

An event that causes the computer program to be diverted from its normal sequence and go to instructions that will respond to the cause. It can be a software instruction or an external signal.

Interrupt Service Routine

A software program that takes action in response to an interrupt.

I/O

Input/Output — Refers to the circuitry of a computer used to bring in or send out data.

IRQ

A signal pin on the microprocessor that, when pulled low by external hardware, will interrupt the normal program sequencing and cause a service routine to be entered.

Jump

An instruction that diverts the program flow from its in-line sequence.

Label

An alpha-numeric symbol used to

identify a certain point in a program.

Least Significant Bits | The binary digits in a digital word which represent values of 0, 1, 2, etc.

Link | The process of combining modular sections of program code. The Microcomputer Development System uses a linker program for this purpose.

Listing | One of the outputs of the assembler which shows the address locations of the machine code as well as the programmers mnemonics and comments.

Load | The process of bringing data into the MPU registers from memory, or into memory from a disk.

Logic Element | A part of a semiconductor circuit used to perform a function such as AND, OR, INVERT, etc.

Logic Levels | The signal line voltage levels that have been defined to represent logic **1s** or **0s**. (2.0 to 5.25 volts = **1**, 0 to 0.8 Volts = **0**).

Look-up-table	A table of values in computer memory that are used to translate information or to define a limit.
Loop	A section of program that branches back and repeats itself until the branch test conditions change.
LOW	One of two possible states of a digital signal. Usually approximately equal to zero volts.
Machine Code	The patterns of **1s** and **0s** in a program that can be interpreted by the microprocessor as instructions.
Mask	A control bit that inhibits an operation, if it is SET.
Memory Map	A drawing or listing of a computer's address space, showing the locations of specific memory or I/O devices.

Millisecond	One thousandth of a second.
Millivolt	One thousandth of a volt.
Mnemonics	An abbreviated word or acronym that helps a programmer remember a function when using Assembly Language.
Module	A functional unit of circuitry (such as a PC card with electronic components), or of a program.
Monitor Program	A program usually in ROM used in a system to provide terminal interface and debugging functions.
Motherboard	The mounting board in a computer chassis used to interconnect the plug-in modules.
MPU	Microprocessing Unit — Heart of a microcomputer.
Octal	A number system with a base of 8.
Offset	A numerical value representing

the difference between two addresses.

ORG   An Assembler Directive used to establish a beginning address.

Parallel   Usually refers to a simultaneous byte-wide transfer of data.

Parity   A method of error detection used with 7-bit data where all words are made to have an even number of 1s, or, alternatively, an odd number.

Pascal   A high-level programming language.

Patch   A new section of machine language code used to fix a programming error. Usually it is located outside the normal code sequence. Normally accessed by a jump instruction.

PC   The Program Counter register of a computer. Also, an abbreviation for Printed Circuit.

PIA	The Peripheral Interface Adapter — One of the 6800 family components, used to provide a parallel I/O function.
Pins	The connections used on Integrated Circuits.
Pointer	Usually refers to an address that is used in an index register to "point to" a byte.
Port	An Input or Output data connection to a system.
PTM	Programmable Timer Module — One of the 6800 Family components, which provides three 16-bit programmable counter/timer circuits.
Pull	An instruction to move bytes from the specified stack, at the position of the current stack pointer, to registers. (e.g., **PULU A**)
Push	An instruction used to save register data on a specified stack at the

next available place. (e.g., **PSHS X,B)**

ROM   Read-Only-Memory — An inte-
                   grated circuit manufactured with
                   a fixed set of user defined instruc-
                   tions.

RAM   Random Access Memory — Tem-
                   porary Read/Write storage for in-
                   formation.

RDRF   Receive Data Register Full — A
                   flag bit in the ACIA that indicates
                   that a character has been received.

READ   To cause data to be brought into
                   the MPU from memory or an I/O
                   device.

Register   A storage location in a micropro-
                   cessor or I/O component.

R/W Memory   Same as RAM.

RESET   To clear a memory or device (store
                   a **0)**, or to preset the system hard-
                   ware.

RS232C — Electronic Industries Association (EIA) specification for serial communication interface.

SBC — Single Board Computer — Used to describe a variety of printed circuit board assemblies made by various manufacturers which contain all elements of a computer on one board.

Serial — Usually refers to data sent bit by bit on one line.

SET — To insert a 1 in a memory.

Setpoints — A high and low limit value set into a Process Control System by an operator or another computer.

Signed Number — A two's complement number. A 1 in the MSB indicates a negative number.

Source — Another name for the Assembly Language program.

Stack — RAM locations that are used to

store temporary data such as the register contents or return addresses.

Store   The process of sending data from the MPU registers into memory.

Subroutine   A modular part of a program. Usually small and ends in an RTS instruction.

SYMbug09   An EXORciser program used for Debugging code distinguished by its use of Symbols (or Labels) instead of absolute addresses. It has the capability to disassemble object code.

Syntax   The organized way that an Instruction must be written so the Assembler Program will recognize it.

Synchronous   Coincidence in time of different events. Controlled by a stable clock signal in a computer.

Thermocouple   A device that changes its electrical output with temperature.

TTL   Transistor-Transistor Logic — A

standardized family of digital ICs designed to work with a 5 volt power supply.

TTL level Signal

A voltage between 2.0 and 5.25 is called a 1 or HIGH and a voltage between 0.0 and 0.8 is a 0 or LOW.

Two's Complement

A binary numbering system in which the most significant bit indicates the polarity (1 for a negative number).

Two-State

Binary or Digital conditions. 1 or 0, HIGH or LOW.

User Map

One of two memory maps of an EXORciser.

Vector

An address in one location that indirectly points to a section of the program.

Weight

The value of a digit determined by its position.

WRITE

To cause data to be sent from the MPU to memory or to an I/O device.

INDEX

A

O

Octal, 6, 168
Offset, 111, 168
ORG, 126, 169

P

Parallel I/O, 10, 12, 169 (see also Peripheral Interface
    Adapter)
Parity, 83, 105, 169
Pascal, 88, 169
Patch (software), 108–112, 169
Peripheral Interface Adapter (PIA), 12, 16, 47–51, 170
    programming of, 70–74, 81, 82, 116–124
Port, 45, 47–48, 52, 70, 82–84, 170
Printer, 62, 63
Programmable Timer Module (PTM), 45, 50, 51, 170
    programming of, 75–80
Pull, 98, 170
Push, 98, 170

R

Random Access Memory (RAM), 2–3, 7–11, 16, 62–63,
    171
Read, 10, 171
Read Only Memory (ROM), 2–3, 8, 10, 171
Register, 8, 10, 12–13, 171
    Condition Code (CCR), 91–97, 159
    of 6809, 97

U

V

W

ABOUT THE AUTHORS

BILL WRAY is an Engineering Section Manager responsible for systems design assurance at Motorola Microsystems, Tempe, Arizona. Previously, he was an Engineering Manager at Raytheon, and a project engineer and Program Manager at TRW. Mr. Wray has made presentations on microcomputers, the Relay Satellite program, and a project in the Apollo program involving lunar ground stations. He has been a member of the Institute of Electrical and Electronics Engineers, Acoustical Society of America, and Society of Motion Picture and Television Engineers.

BILL CRAWFORD is a Microcomputer Applications Engineer at Motorola Microsystems. Previously, he was a design engineer and project leader on various NASA projects for the Motorola Government Electronics Division, design engineer on the BOMARC Weapon Control System in the Missile Division of Boeing Airplane Co., and a radar and navigation instructor in the United States Air Force. Mr. Crawford has presented numerous papers at several major electronics conferences.